ECONOMIC DOCTRINE AND METHOD

AAKAR BOOKS CLASSICS

ECONOMIC DOCTRINE AND METHOD

An Historical Sketch

Joseph A. Schumpeter

AAKAR

Economic Doctrine and Method: An Historical Sketch
Joseph A. Schumpeter

First Published 1954
First Aakar Edition 2020
Reprinted 2024

ISBN 978-93-5002-645-8

Published by
AAKAR BOOKS
28 E Pocket IV, Mayur Vihar Phase I
Delhi 110 091, India
www.aakarbooks.com

Printed at
Mudrak, Noida

TRANSLATOR'S FOREWORD

In presenting this early work by the late Professor Schumpeter to the English-speaking public, I am deeply conscious of the limitations which are imposed on anybody who attempts to express ideas that have been given literary form in one language, through the medium of another. Every language has its own peculiar structure and follows its own laws and it is well known that it would be fatal to try to force this structure on to a different language. Words have not only definite meanings as such, they also have allusive and associationist qualities which are bound to disappear in translation. Moreover, in a curious and perhaps not yet completely analysed way, thought not only directs and employs language but language itself determines thought.

There are a great many words in every language which cannot be reproduced in another except with the help of lengthy and often wearisome explanations. Words like 'Geisteswissenschaft', 'Sozialpolitik', 'Verelendung' and numerous others have no exact equivalent in English. In addition, the structure of a German sentence is so fundamentally different from that of an English sentence that a literal translation would appear clumsy and often downright ridiculous.

I have, of course, attempted throughout to convey faithfully the meaning intended by the author and at the same time to make the book as readable as possible. In order to achieve this result I have eliminated or transcribed all such metaphors as would mean nothing to the English reader. I have broken up sentences into shorter phrases and I have used far more paragraphs than the original contains.

If nevertheless I have not wholly succeeded in making this translation read like an original piece of writing, it is because that could only have been achieved if large parts of the book had been completely re-written. It must be remembered that this book was composed before the First World War and that it was meant in the first place for German economists. Its extensive bibliography, which I have taken over entirely in the form in which the author presented it to his public, covers publications only up to 1912. That a translation is still insistently demanded, despite this lapse of time, speaks sufficiently of the enduring value of Professor Schumpeter's work.

R. ARIS

BIBLIOGRAPHICAL PREFACE[1]

Serious interest in the history of Political Economy did not develop until the classical system decayed. Although some bibliographies had been compiled in the eighteenth century only relatively little historical work had been done. Rossig's *Versuch einer Geschichte der Oekonomie und Kameralwissenschaft*, 1781, should be mentioned in this connection. Even during the first decades of the nineteenth century it was chiefly in Germany that scholars devoted themselves to this work: for example Weitzel's *Geschichte der Staatswissenschaften*, 1832-3, Baumstark's *Cameralistische Encyclopädie*, 1835, and von Mohl's *Geschichte und Literatur der Staatswissenschaften*, 1855–8. McCulloch's *The Literature of Political Economy*, 1845, was a brief catalogue with short notes and was valuable as such.

The book by Blanqui *Histoire de L'économie politique en Europe*, 1838, was very successful; it was the first attempt to produce a genuine history of our science, although it was rather superficial. The book by Kautz *Geschichtliche Entwicklung der Nationalökonomie und ihrer Literatur*, 1860, is of similar calibre and was far surpassed by the main work on the history of economic doctrine written by his teacher Roscher, *Geschichte der Nationalökonomie in Deutschland*, 1874. The latter was the result of the most diligent research and set the standard for a long time; it is worth reading even today in spite of some of its shortcomings. This is also true of the same writer's book: *Geschichte der englischen Volkswirtschaftslehre*, 1851. Nevertheless in vigour of presentation and mastery of the ideas described Dühring's *Kritische Geschichte der Nationalökonomie und des Sozialismus*, 1874, is far superior to Roscher's work.

Since then a survey of the whole history of Economics of equal importance has not been attempted in Germany. Eisenhart's *Geschichte der Nationalökonomie*, 1881, is devoted almost entirely to

[1] We are confining ourselves here to the literature on the history of economic doctrine, excluding that on sociological doctrine. Further, the catalogue in the text is limited to publications which cover or intend to cover the whole material, or at least its greater part for the period in question.

ideas in the field of social policy. The solid study by Oncken: *Geschichte der Nationalökonomie*, 1902, deals only with the period before Adam Smith. A short survey of the history of methods and systems can be found in v. Schmoller's article 'Volkswirtschaftslehre' in the *Handwörterbuch der Staatswissenschaften*. In addition we may mention Scheel's article on the history of doctrine in Schönberg's *Handbuch der politischen Oekonomie*, the symposium *Die geschichtliche Entwicklung der deutschen Volkswirtschaftslehre*, 1908, and Hasbach's work which form the raw material for a large-scale history of Economics. French literature is richer in works of a summarizing character. Apart from the works of Espinas, Rambaud and Dubois there is the outstanding book by Gide and Rist, *Histoire des doctrines économiques*, 1908. Denis' uncompleted *Histoire des systèmes économiques et socialistes*, 1904–07, was planned on a larger scale. English literature can produce only one solid achievement in this field: Ingram's *History of Political Economy*, 1888 (German translation, 2nd. ed. 1905).[1] American literature possesses a textbook in Haney's *History of Economic Thought*, 1911. Cossa's book *Guida allo Studio dell' economica politica*, although it had a great success, cannot be given very high marks. Among the histories of Economics in various countries we may mention the relevant articles in Palgrave's *Dictionary of Political Economy*. Roscher's *History of German Economics* also affords glimpses into other countries. The only periodical devoted to the history of doctrine is in French: *Revue d'histoire des doctrines économiques*, Paris.

Specialized research in the field of the history of doctrines must of course be looked for in the first place in specialized works about individual authors and schools. Of these only a few can be mentioned in the following section. Yet from the history of individual doctrines and problems, in which full justice can be done to the historical evolution in all its details, we can learn far more

[1] J. Bonar must be mentioned here in the same sense as, say, Hasbach. He also exploited his great knowledge in various individual contributions in which he illuminated large sections of our science. His main work is *Philosophy and Political Economy in some of their Historical Relations*, 1893 (2nd ed., 1909).

than from comprehensive histories and monographs. We mention above all: v. Böhm Bawerk, *Kapital und Kapitalzins*, vol. I, *Geschichte und Kritik der Kapitalzinstheorieen*, 1st ed. 1884, 2nd ed. 1902. Marx: *Theorien über den Mehrwert* (ed. Kautsky), Zuckerkandl, *Zur Theorie des Preises*, 1889. Whittaker, *History and Criticism of the Labour Theory of Value in English Political Economy*, 1903. Liebknecht, *Zur Geschichte der Werttheorie in England*, 1902. Sewall, *The Theory of Value Before A. Smith*, 1901. Kaulla, *Die Geschichtliche Entwicklung der modernen Werttheorieen*, 1906. Graziani, *Storia critica della teoria del valore*, 1889. Salz, *Beiträge zur Geschichte und Kritik der Lohnfondstheorie*, 1905. v. Bergmann, *Geschichte der nationalökonomischen Krisentheorieen*, 1899. F. Hoffmann, *Kritische Geschichte der Geldwerttheorie*. Rost, *Die Wert- und Preistheorie mit Berücksichtigung ihrer dogmengeschichtlichen Entwicklung*, 1908. Pierstorff, *Unternehmergewinn*. Mataja, *Unternehmergewinn*. A. Menger, *Recht auf den vollen Arbeitsertrag*. Zwiedinek, *Lohntheorie und Lohnpolitik*. Ergang, *Untersuchungen zum Maschinenproblem*. Kostanecki, *Arbeit und Armut* and many others.

These histories of doctrines and the critical reviews devoted to them are of very unequal value but they are nevertheless attempts at a genuinely scientific treatment of ideas. In a wider sense it would be possible to place here almost our entire literature as almost every author offers surveys and reviews in the field of doctrinal history.

CONTENTS

I

THE DEVELOPMENT OF ECONOMICS AS A SCIENCE[1]

The science of economics, as it took shape towards the end of the eighteenth century, had grown from two roots which must be clearly differentiated from one another. The great writings of the eighteenth century of which Adam Smith's *Wealth of Nations* is by far the most important example, epitomized the work of previous writers and handed it down to posterity. They offer us two strands of thought that had long existed independently of each other. One of these strands originated in the study of the philosophers in the widest sense of the term, that is, those thinkers to whom social activities as such appeared as the fundamental problem and as an essential element in their conception of the world. This strand derived therefore from Philosophy as the great mother of all sciences. The other had been accumulated by people of various types whose primary motive had been their interest in practical

[1] Literature: Of special works Hasbach's *Philosophische Grundlagen der von F. Quesnay and A. Smith begründeten Politischen Oekonomie*, Schmoller's *Forschungen*, 1890, and Bonar's above-mentioned book are of particular importance. The economy of classical antiquity can be studied best in the general literature on classical subjects, particularly that on ancient economic history. We may, however, mention two works on Aristotle's economic views. Kraus, *Wertlehre des Aristoteles*, and Kinkel, *Sozialökonomische Anschauungen des Aristoteles*. Compare also: Gouchon, *Les doctrines économiques dans la Grèce antique*. For the remainder of this epoch: Endemann, *Studien in der romanisch-kanonistischen Wirtschafts-und Rechtslehre*. Ashley, *English Economic History and Theory*. Contzen, *Geschichte der volkswirtschaftlichen Literatur im Mittelalter*. Brants, *Theories économiques au XIII et XIV siècles*. Laspeyres, *Geschichte der volkswirtschaftlichen Anschauungen der Niederländer und ihrer Literatur zur Zeit der Republik*, 1865. Gargas, *Die volkswirtschaftlichen Anschauungen in Polen im XVII. Jahrh.* Small, *The Cameralists*. Leslie Stephen, *English Thought in the Eighteenth Century*. Supino, *La scienza economica in Italia nei secoli XVI-XVII* (1888). Horn, *L'économie politique avant les physiocrats*, 1867.

problems of the day. It is the intention of the present writer to trace the genesis of these two strands, even though this must of necessity be done somewhat briefly. It must also be borne in mind that in some cases this division, however essential, tends to break down when applied to the facts, as any such classification occasionally does, and is then bound to appear as an arbitrary one.

The 'philosophic' strand has its ultimate literary base in the thought of Ancient Greece and can clearly be distinguished from the conceptions of everyday life and the principles of legislators and founders of religions. This is true not only in the sense that the Greek thinkers expressed ideas of an economic character which in later years were to be formulated again independently, but also in the sense that the Greeks themselves influenced posterity. Thus an uninterrupted, or at least continuously reconnected, chain of references led from them to most of the authors from whom the works of Adam Smith derived, and finally to Smith himself. The Greek influences which are most important for us are those of Aristotle, Plato, the Stoics and Epicureans, if we put them in the order in which they have significance for us. The value of what they had to offer must not, however, be over-estimated, apart from its historical significance. It would be a mistake to interpret every chance utterance in the sense which later thinkers have attached to similarly sounding statements. Moreover, certain fundamental statements which stand at the threshold of economic theory are so simple and derive so naturally from the practical and half-instinctive knowledge of economic processes that their formulation cannot be considered as a particularly memorable achievement.

Finally, the ancient thinkers gave very much less attention to specifically economic problems than to, say, those of political science, while in later years relatively more work was done on the former than on the latter with which the ancients had been primarily concerned. For these two reasons the Greek legacy is of smaller significance in the field of economics than in others. It is not true, as has often been maintained, that the economy of the 'oikos' with its autarky of the household produced no problems of a 'political' economy proper, and the 'oikos' economy was not quite so prevalent as is assumed in this argument. Nevertheless it is true that scientific thought in the sphere of economic life did not develop very far. The historians offer us even less as far as an insight into economic principles is concerned. Even the best amongst them are altogether surprisingly weak when it comes to generalizations. The brilliant ingenuity which Thucydides, e.g., displays whenever he judges individual events seems to desert him when he discusses general causes and consequences, while he hardly touches on specifically economic problems. The literature of the orators and dramatists contains in no case more than what might be described as the expression of popular conceptions.

Even Aristotle and Plato presented an exceedingly poor and above all 'pre-scientific' picture of economics; it does not differ substantially from that of laymen of all ages. There is no question of any insight into the mutual relations between economic phenomena. Their examination of the various economic functions reflects the attitude of an aristocracy which is confronted by a rising merchant class and has essentially an agrarian outlook. Nevertheless, if everything is taken into account, Aristotle's contribution in the field of economic is considerable. The following are its most important points:

1. Although he always valued economic actions in ethical terms he was the first and for a long time the only thinker to recognize that the economic activity of man represents a problem of intrinsic interest distinguished clearly and incisively from mere household and workshop management on the one hand and from the art of the legislator, on the other. This represented a particularly great achievement since the Greek thinkers in general understood by economics almost exclusively the kind of practical economic knowledge as offered by Xenophon or even by the book on economics which has come to be included among Aristotle's works. Besides, the Greeks normally occupied themselves with economic problems merely from the point of view of the art of the legislator or with a view to the construction of an ideal State. Only in Aristotle's writings do we find a somewhat more elaborate train of thought of an inquiring and analytical character, so that he must be described as the creator of that first strand of thought distinguished above. In one particular passage he already defined economics as

the science of 'wealth' (Nic. Ethics, p. 1094) and he, in general, assigned it roughly to the place which it was to occupy in the system of moral philosophy and natural law as it was developed in the eighteenth century.

2. Aristotle laid the foundations for a theory of value and price. He recognized the significance of a distinction between value in use and value in exchange and thus clearly grasped the problem inherent in this distinction. The doctrine of the exchange value became to him the pivot of a theory of market economics (chrematistics). As he based this theory on the fact of human wants, he arrived at a purely subjective theory of economic value and though he maintained the supremacy of ethical laws, he developed a theory of price as well, without however offering a real explanation for the phenomenon of price. This led him to his classical statement on the nature and function of money as a means of exchange and measurement of value. (Pol. I, 9 and Ethics, V 8). How deeply he grasped the fundamental importance of these matters appeared from the fact that he based his conception of economic commodities upon the measurability of their value in terms of money. Even Pufendorf's store of economic theorems still lies within this outline.

3. He clearly distinguished between money and wealth and employed arguments which were later to serve in the fight against mercantilism. Elsewhere, when he for instance stresses the special character of those production goods which are used for further earnings, and therefore employed a definition of capital which is still customary today, he reveals an attitude which might easily induce us to ascribe to him a very far-reaching measure of economic insight. On the whole, however, such approximations to modern theory are isolated and are often followed by examples of gross errors.

4. Aristotle's theory of interest which is of such historical importance cannot be counted amongst these gross errors. It is true that his conception of production is primitive and encompasses merely the element of material productivity. In consequence, profits produced by trade seemed to him explicable merely as a result of fraud. The argument of the 'unproductivity' of money, how-

ever, is not so erroneous as is sometimes assumed, if one considers the case of loans for consumption, which are indeed the only ones that Aristotle takes into account.

5. Furthermore, Aristotle, in a calm and objective manner, started those discussions on social institutions, such as private property and slavery, from the point of view of their social usefulness. These indeed still play their part even in the economic literature of today.

6. Finally, he laid the foundations for a science of sociology. From the beginning he fought against a purely individualistic approach, even though he employed somewhat scholastic arguments. He attempted to grasp the character of the phenomenon of society from the point of view of the social psychologist in a manner which has influenced the entire literature of social philosophy and hence, also, that of economics. In particular, he laid the foundations for the theory of the inherent sociability of men living together, which Grotius was to develop fully. Occasionally (e.g., Pol. II, 6, 13) when he talks as a social reformer he assumes an attitude which strikes us as entirely modern.

A whole world separates these achievements from the highly coloured phantoms in Plato's thought. The latter offers us neither precise conceptions of an economic character nor sustained analytical arguments. His aim was not to explain an economy which was problematic in itself but to create an economic order which was adapted to his ethical principles and to the conditions that prevailed in his ideal State. It is probably true that this was partly merely a form which he chose in order to present scientific ideas, but even his pronouncements on the division of labour (Republic II), to which reference is always being made, afford little proof that he possessed a deeper insight into the sphere of economics. Even Xenophon (Kyr. VIII) was easily his superior in this respect while the rest of his economic statements and arguments are those of the layman. The dialogue Eryxias contains a more forceful attempt to rise above the ideas of the layman in the field of economics and represents an analysis of basic economic conceptions superior to Plato's writings.

The Stoics or Epicureans offer us even less positive insight into economic questions while, as Hasbach has emphasized, their influence on the intellectual work of the philosophers, first in ancient Rome and later in the world of the Renaissance, was so much the greater. Moreover, since from the earliest times thinkers have played with sociological conceptions, it is understandable that these philosophical systems too had to some extent a sociological character. Yet we must be on our guard against overrating the significance of this factor for our subject. Above all, neither the Stoics nor the Epicureans approached the problems in our way. Their individualist attitude amounted hardly to more than the advice to keep away from public life. In consequence, there is no connection whatever between their individualism and the kind of individualism with which we are alone concerned, namely, individualism as a principle of social science and as a starting point for social research. Furthermore, the teachings of Epicurus have in fact as little in common with the Eudaimonism of our times as the doctrines of the Stoics have with modern tendencies of social ethics. In this respect it is particularly easy to be deceived by superficial similarities and to perceive the germs for scientific social insight in these philosophic systems just as later thinkers tended to clothe essentially new ideas in a terminology which they had derived from the ancients. These achievements later affected the science of economics in two ways. First of all, in the course of time they were passed on from one thinker to another. Roman and medieval thinkers adopted them and from them they were taken over by more modern scholars. Second, with the coming of the Renaissance and, long after, the Greek thinkers themselves became a living force and developed into teachers of the modern thinkers who turned to them directly as well.

Even today it is difficult, and in some respects downright impossible to discuss economics without considering its sister disciplines. As long as the store of specifically economic knowledge was small, and economics merely a small component part of the great universal science of philosophy, this separation was still more difficult. Nevertheless, if we want to keep within the framework of the present book, we are forced to try to do so. For this reason let it be briefly stated that in ancient Rome the store of knowledge did not increase. This goes without saying as far as philosophy and historiography were concerned, which indeed were completely unoriginal, and as regards Jurisprudence perhaps nothing else could be expected. We see how lawyers approach problems of economic life with the greatest confidence, but this is merely the assurance of the experienced businessman, while the very purpose of legal argumentation with its inherent limitations makes economic controversies impossible. Occasional statements like the famous definition of price by Paulus were isolated and thence signify very little, and thus we can understand that modern researches into the economic doctrines of the 'Corpus Juris' had not produced any results as far as our problems are concerned (v. Scheel, Oertmann). The manuals on husbandry of those authors who wrote *de re rustica* likewise offer nothing in the form of economic knowledge: this fact which is so much more striking as there would have been no lack of problems in the sphere of land reform, as vital as those of England in the eighteenth and nineteenth centuries.

For the next instalment of speculative thought about economic problems—speculative as opposed to popular ideas and to the conceptions of isolated men in 'business'—we shall naturally turn to scholasticism. In fact, we discover that in this respect as in others scholasticism follows Aristotle as closely as for instance Marx followed Ricardo. Although its main purpose was often in the nature of moral casuistry we must not be blind to the fact that the cases under discussion and the religious commandments are as often as not merely the outward form of objective research which sometimes impresses us the more favourably the longer we study it.

In the field of economics, however, this seems to be the case only to a limited extent and the value of the statements of the scholastics appears to be small. In connection with the ethical problem of the just price we find the beginnings of a theory of price, first formulated as far as we know to any considerable extent by Albertus Magnus (1193–1280). Magnus tried to give to Aristotle's ideas about price a more precise form by stating that equality of the amounts of *labores et expensa* contained in goods to be exchanged would form an ideal criterion for the exchange relation. This statement, however, is made merely as a moral postulate and is even derived from another moral postulate which forbade unfair trade. Above all, it stands completely without any relation to those ideas that might have made it eventually serviceable in economic theory. This is an example for many of the economic arguments produced by the Scholastics. While most of them, and amongst them even Thomas Aquinas, did not produce any original ideas in this field, a tendency developed—starting perhaps with Duns Scotus—to make utility of commodities the basis for an explanation of the exchange economy. This tendency led Buridan[1] in the first half of the fourteenth century to the formulation of a theory of money which, elaborated by Oresmius, represents probably the first purely economic achievement. Its fundamental conception, which based the value of money on the use value of its material, never again disappeared. This whole tendency culminated towards the end of the fifteenth century with Gabriel Biel who is usually considered to have brought the period of scholasticism to a close. Yet scholasticism handed on its heritage in the field of social science to the school of the Law of Nature.

One of the consequences, more precisely a special application, of the price theory of the scholastics was their theory of interest. In it an attempt was made to provide a theoretical basis for the well-known approach of medieval thinkers to the question of charging interest. This theory of interest survived until the latter part of the eighteenth century. It served as perhaps the most important theme for discussions of purely economic problems which constantly opened up new vistas. The remaining achievements of this school cannot be dealt with here. Further, it goes without saying that it would be possible to derive from the complex of scholastic ideas an integrated picture of economics, but this picture was not the result of conscious research but merely the reflection of the general attitude to current problems.

This small stream of intellectual achievements in the field of social science flowed into the stormy sea of ideas during the period of the Renaissance and the Reformation. From among the confusion of its currents which defy description owing to limitations of

[1] Kaulla, *Der Lehrer des Oresmius*, Tübinger Zeitschrift, 1904.

space imposed upon us two may be mentioned. First, the general intellectual tendency in the sphere of social science derived from the impetus produced by the political, religious and social revolutions of the period. This tendency led numerous new workers into this field who viewed State and society from new points of view.

Secondly, the current which was released directly by the awakening of the spirit of the natural sciences but indirectly derived from the same impetus. It is true that this period clearly shows its historical continuity with scholasticism and that its achievements never shed certain external forms of scholastic thought, while on the other hand the new fermentation gradually changed the thought of social science into something quite different.

With the proviso that all such general statements can never be strictly true one can say that the social world accepted by earlier thinkers as a mystery or as self-evident now appeared as an intellectual problem, to be comprehended with natural rather than with supernatural conceptions. These conceptions were to be derived from observation and an analysis of facts based on experience. This rationalization of the social world—in the sense of a rational perception by means of the relation of cause and effect—was attempted methodically by analysing the 'reasonable' motives of human actions on which society is obviously based, or even by declaring certain social aims as reasonable. Strictly speaking these meanings of the word 'rationalist' have nothing whatsoever to do with each other. The historian who explains the dissolution of the Spanish Empire by its inherent lack of vitality attempts to explain the event and rationalizes it by applying the relation of cause and effect. It must not be assumed, however, that because of this he sees the social world merely as the resultant of reasonable motives on the part of its acting members. He certainly does not for that matter consider certain conditions of society as absolutely reasonable. The term 'Rationalism', however, has become a catchword in which these meanings, and incidentally others as well, have become mixed. In order to penetrate into the essence of rationalism in the sphere of social science it is imperative for us to stress the fact that up to the time of the rise of historiography in the eighteenth century these different meanings generally flow together in the minds of the thinkers. This happened often, though to an ever diminishing degree, right up to modern times. It was understandable that the first thinkers in this field, when they wanted to comprehend social activities, turned to the reasoning mind of the actors for an explanation and considered any 'unreasonable' action on principle as an uninteresting aberration. We shall, therefore, understand that on the one side thinkers arrived at an individualist point of view, which saw in the world of motives within the individual the key to an understanding of social problems, while on the other side they maintained that there was an immutable and universally valid order which alone corresponded to Reason. They arrived at these conclusions because it seemed obvious to them that human mentality was something unchangeably established and in consequence that the law of action derived from it was in a certain sense equally unchangeable, as was its creation, the social world. In this can be found the origin of individualism in science and at the same time of the conception of general normal conditions of society which, however, did not exist in reality and had to be established for this very reason. Let us, however, take note that the point from which these thinkers started was even in the modern sense a strictly scientific one and that the idea of basing social science on psychology represents a line of thought which today has gained renewed vigour. Deterred by superficialities and by the obvious defects of this literature we are apt to forget today how completely our own work rests on the same foundations.[1]

[1] It is usual to see individualism and rationalism primarily as a social philosophy. It is, however, more important for us to stress the fact that an individualist and rationalist way of thinking offered itself to the inquiring mind as the one most natural, that it lay, as it were, on the path of scientific progress. Moreover, it is usual to attach an unjustifiable importance to theological formulations. It is indeed true that this entire period thought in theological terms, but it is necessary to distinguish between a way of thinking which explains phenomena in supernatural terms and an approach which within the framework of science offers us 'natural' causes and insists merely that all things correspond to a higher will or plan. In the latter case the argumentation is entirely positive and scientific. Only in this sense do we find the 'theological element in Descartes, Locke, Newton and so on, and it has no longer a real influence on the results'. The same is true in our field. The theological form is being preserved long after thought in the sphere of social science has in fact wholly emancipated itself.

At first there developed a 'rationalist' theology which in itself is of little significance for us but which is indirectly of great importance. In this connection we observe with the deepest interest how, when the discussion first started with the controversies of the Reformation, it still relied entirely upon the old means of interpretation. Later, however, this method is dropped completely and replaced by an analysis of the facts of religious consciousness until the various forms of Deism were reached. This Deism corresponds exactly to the eternal but 'natural' law, that is to say, it is a faith arrived at with the help of 'Reason' but with a definitely determined content and it is not a doctrine of the general nature and the social function of religious faith as such. All thinkers of the period have touched on these problems. Even Adam Smith still lectured on 'Natural Theology', but this theme is already separated not only from the subject matter of social science but from the rest of philosophy. Even some purely theological writers like Butler influenced thought in the field of social science deeply.

Later on from the mother-science of theological philosophy an independent Ethics detached itself which stood in close relation to political economy, and displays the same analytical—and this means in this context psychological—tendency. It was already a genuine social science and had never lost touch with economics in spite of statements to the contrary which have been so popular. The ethical system of this period based ethical phenomena also on general explanatory principles such as Shaftesbury's moral sense, or the principle of sympathy maintained by Adam Smith, or that of identification of morals and positive legislation in the writings of Hobbes, or on even more distinct echoes of ancient ideas in Grotius, or on Mandeville's principle of egoism, to name only a few of importance to us. In this case also we observe the transition from theological discussion to a 'scientific' conception to which we have already referred, notwithstanding the theological cloak which even most of the later thinkers never discarded. Here, too, we find the yearning for moral knowledge with a concrete content, but we must distinguish it from the basic desire for knowledge and explanation in the widest sense.

The doctrine of Natural Law which in the sixteenth century

grew into an independent discipline is of still greater importance to us. It is very difficult to give an adequate idea of the extent of scientific progress made within its framework. In the circles of Italian and French lawyers who at first were still working with the tools of the Postglossatores, that is, were using the method of casuistry and exegesis, a critical spirit developed early under the favourable influence of the circumstances outlined above, so that they questioned the content of the legal systems with which they dealt. This critical spirit was ultimately derived from the natural sciences of Greece which had been made known through Arab intermediaries.[1]

Slowly there grew from this with ever increasing strength the idea of a Law which existed outside any concrete legislation; a Law which was derived from the elements of human nature as they were known by experience and from the innermost needs of society. Gradually a positive science of law, and, as its basis, a science of State and society unfolded itself, partly under the tutelage of the French doctrine of the 'dual truth' which secured to scientific thought a considerable independence while it formally acknowledged the supremacy of religious doctrine. This science lost nothing of its character as a science based on experience, although its data—already faulty in themselves—fell far short of the far-reaching conclusions that had been based upon them. The theological phraseology, however, and the fact that until the eighteenth century the scientific aim of a theory of the general nature of law appeared to the inquiring minds always in the fantastic form of a plan to discover a generally valid system of concrete legal rules, made it difficult for critics to recognize the true character of the Law of Nature and in consequence to appreciate its greatness. All this has led to the well-known prejudices against any speculations on the theme of Natural Law.

It is difficult to select the names of those that ought to be mentioned here. As we deal with economics it is natural that those

[1] Even as far as Aristotle was concerned, only the Arts subjects had become alive and effective amongst the scholastics. Greek natural sciences had been neglected or even completely misunderstood and became influential only through the Arabs.

authors must be considered in the first place who contributed most economic knowledge proper. This is true above all of the Physiocrats who can already be classed as having been preponderantly concerned with economics and whose doctrine will have to occupy us later on. Apart from them it was Pufendorf[1] who has influenced our discipline most directly, whose economic theses formed the nucleus for those of Hutcheson, and who, in consequence, contributed an essential part of the doctrine of Hutcheson's disciple, Adam Smith. We must also mention Locke whose economic achievements, however, stands somewhat apart from his other conceptions in the field of Natural Law. While it is impossible to discuss here the importance for our discipline of Oldendorp, Grotius, Gassendi, Bodius, Cardano, Hobbes and others, it is necessary to talk briefly about Hutcheson because of his relation to the *Wealth of Nations*. His *System of Moral Philosophy* is for us the most important book written by this Glasgow professor (d. 1761). It was, although published in 1755, essentially the fruit of his lecturing activities concluded in 1746 and contains a very comprehensive theory of economics. (Compare W. R. Scott, *Francis Hutcheson*, 1900.) It is quite obvious that the doctrines of the division of labour, of value, price and money have substantially been taken over by Adam Smith. In particular, it must be noticed that to Hutcheson labour appeared as the measure of exchange value as it did to all writers of the classical school. In his theory of distribution there emerged clearly the naive over-estimation of the physical productivity of land which is also displayed in the system of the Physiocrats. From this he derived in part his theory of interest—developed once more twenty-one years later by Turgot. On the other hand, however, Hutcheson based income from interest on the profit of the entrepreneur gained with the help of the borrowed money—in this he approaches Locke's position—while A. Smith avoids this conclusion. He also recognized clearly the significance of those factors that were later to become so important, as the

[1] H. Conring was a very poor economist and Thomasius and Wolff cannot be classified as economists at all. In the case of the two latter there can be no question of a deep insight, or even a vivid interest, in the subject, except that they showed some concern for problems of public finance and policy.

famous phrase of 'Supply and Demand'. As regards international trade Hutcheson stands half-way between mercantilist ideas and those of Adam Smith. He essentially completed the process already noticeable in Pufendorf's work of separating social science from theology and, lastly his basic social conceptions clearly reveal a utilitarian tendency.

We must further draw attention to three points. First, one trend within the school of Natural Law gradually led to the theory of Utilitarianism with which later the name of Bentham became associated. At first this simply meant that the element of social utility was emphasized in a certain direction. The result of this, however, was that the key to social action was sought in the will of the individual, in his desire to seek pleasure and to avoid pain. This was to be of the greatest importance, especially in economics, to which this conception was suited best, while it was rather ineffective outside its province. It was an efficient instrument of economic analysis and resulted, partly directly, partly through the stimulus which it gave to criticism, in a considerable extension of knowledge in the field of social science. Secondly, we may stress the fact that the idea of the social contract was simultaneously developed and overcome by representatives of the school of Natural Law. We must not condemn this idea because it was historically valuless since many social relations are based, if not on a conscious contract, at least on the fact of mutual services, so that it deserves as a heuristic principle a better treatment than it received from the historians of political thought. This evidently applies particularly to the economic relations of which an economic system is composed, and this idea contributed, consciously or unconsciously, much to a clearer insight in economics, free from metaphysical elements. Thirdly, we like to recall that, as v. Philoppovich (*Die Entwicklung der deutschen Volkswirtschaftslehre*, Festgabe für G. v. Schmoller) has shown, the idea of society and various theories connected with it penetrated into the German economic theory only with the help of the teachers of the Law of Nature during the nineteenth century.

All these special branches—Theology, Ethics, Jurisprudence and Economics—formed a unity for which the term 'Moral Philosophy' became customary. By this we must not understand either a 'moral doctrine' or a 'philosophy' in the modern sense but a comprehensive system of thought (*Geisteswissenschaft*), which in spite of all metaphysical admixture became more and more empirical and analytical and was opposed to the natural sciences, termed in those days Philosophy of Nature. This system of moral philosophy rested in all its branches on identical premises, that is, on the same simple assumptions with regard to human motives and their relation to human actions; it was in all its parts individualistic, rationalist and absolute in the sense that the conception of growth receded almost completely into the background. Since in this organic unity one element affects all the others, almost every thought is of importance for economics as well. In this connection the philosophic achievements of Locke and Hume must be mentioned in the first place, because never again was philosophy to such an extent a social science as at this period. A prominent part must also be assigned to the associationist psychology of Hartley whose basic principles still dominated the thought of J. S. Mill. This psychology was of the greatest importance for the development of economic theory. We cannot go into this question here, however, nor can we deal with phenomena which were outside the broad avenue of sociological thought, such as G. Vico's *Principi di una scienza nuova* (1721).

7. Let us now turn to the second source of our discipline. The thinkers, to whom we have drawn attention so far, approach economic problems from an interest in 'philosophy' in the widest sense of the term and gradually began to pay attention to our sector of the world of phenomena, employing tools that had been shaped elsewhere, and from points of view arrived at in other spheres; on the other hand, for those, whom we must mention now, practical problems and practical aims were of decisive importance, even if in these thinkers also the desire for knowledge for its own sake made itself felt. For most of these thinkers human activity was by no means problematical in itself. They were preponderantly practical men without any specific scientific training and without any inclination to philosophic questioning. A fact had to be doubtful in the eyes of the practical politician in order to appear to them as a question that had to be answered. Moreover, for the solution

of problems which happened to arise they brought along intelligence and experiences of life and of business but no philosophical equipment. Thus it is explained why in this branch of economic literature so many excellent beginnings led to nothing because they were not followed up beyond the concrete controversy which had occasioned them. We also understand why we find side by side with many diagnoses that were clearly and vigorously formulated some primitive prejudices, why it often happened that details were recognized while the underlying principle was missed, and why the analysis never penetrated beyond what the occasion demanded and in most cases did not attempt any clarification of the fundamental issues. In brief, this branch of our literature reveals all the freshness and fruitfulness of direct observation. At the same time it shows all the helplessness of mere observation by itself, at least in the early stages, while gradually from the sphere of chance arguments and current discussions there emerged some attempts to carry out a genuine analysis. Even today we possess such a popular literature, which in many cases does not attain greater heights than did the writings of those days. This can be explained by the lack of prestige enjoyed by strictly scientific knowledge in our sphere. In the earlier period, however, 'popular economics' could contribute much to the budding discipline of scientific economics. Only in so far as it affected and produced scientific knowledge is it of interest to us here, not as a reflection of the prevailing current conditions.

These discussions of striking and from a practical point of view important questions assumed a different character in the various countries. Nowhere else did they flourish so much as they did in England, where political conditions made a strong appeal to the general public, a necessary condition for the success of practical endeavours. In other countries this practical motive was more or less absent, as was the training in parliamentary tradition; an autocratic government discouraged an interest in economic policy. As a result, the foundations for England's supremacy in the realm of economic thought were already laid in the period from 1500 to 1700, and this supremacy became undisputed in the first half of the nineteenth century. Monetary conditions, the policy of enclosure, with the resulting decline of agriculture, the ancient restrictions on traffic imposed by governmental order, the privileges of foreign merchants, the decay of the staple system, especially after the loss of Calais, the rates of exchange, particularly those with Holland, the fight against the trade monopolies, first of royal favourites, later of the great trading companies, the export of wool, considered ruinous by a great many people, the establishment of the banking system: round all these matters literary controversies arose.

Although at first these controversies were dominated by considerations for purely temporary purposes, they led later to a clarification of some points of view, to a vivid desire for economic analysis and, finally, to the establishment of a store of economic conceptions, systems of thought and descriptive knowledge. We may mention as one of the earliest descriptive surveys of current problems from an integrating point of view the treatise by Hales, which according to Lamond (*Eng. Hist. Rev.*, 1891) was written in dialogue form in 1549 and was published in 1581. It bore the title 'A compendious and briefe examination of certayne ordinary complaints of divers of our countrymen in these our dayes', and in it all the discussed 'complaints' about the depreciation of money were attributed to the import of gold and silver from America. The basic views of the author are entirely those of everyday life, his judgments those of a thinking but quite untrained mind. Nevertheless, nothing equally valuable appeared for a long time. The undoubted superiority of systematic analysis and the extent of the progress which we owe to the latter come to our mind when we survey the extremely naïve discussions of problems which were dear to the heart of those successful and experienced businessmen. The demand for governmental regulation of the rates of exchange and the fear of the export of gold offer good examples. It took a long time until the conception was overcome—Milles[1], Malynes and Misselden may be mentioned as its representatives—that the establishment of the rates of exchange depended merely on the behaviour of the merchants directly concerned with the exchange

[1] As a result of an irreparable error I could not make myself familiar with this author in the original.

transaction, a conception which is shared by many a layman even today. Great progress was made when this 'bullionist' conception was given up and people realized instead that exchange rates and the balance of trade were correlated. As far as this happened—the change becomes apparent to us with complete clarity in Maddison's *England is Looking In and Out*, 1640—research into the factors which in their turn influenced the balance of trade came to the fore; this research then led to a deeper understanding of economic transactions. The clear and well set out treatise by Mun, *England's Treasure by Forraign Trade*, 1664, which was eminently convincing to the practical businessman, became epoch-making. Without any scientific merit this work in a very precise and fortunate manner gave expression to the views on economic policy that were held by a great many people. Among the contemporaries and successors of Mun we must particularly mention Sir Josiah Child, *Brief Observations Concerning trade and the Interest of Money*, 1668, *The British Merchant*, 1721, and Gee, *Trade and Navigation of Great Britain Considered*, 1729, whose books are well worth reading as examples of a primitive economic theory and of the way in which it grew into a scientific system of economics. This tendency prevailed throughout the greater part of the eighteenth century and culminated in the much more penetrating work by Sir James Stewart, *Inquiry into the Principles of Political Economy*, 1767. His scientific importance, however, is based on different influences.[1]

With the exception of the latter all these authors share the characteristic feature that they adopted the basic ideas of everyday life uncritically and try to decide certain questions merely with their help. In the second half of the seventeenth century, however, a period which the historian Hallam once described as the nadir of England's national prosperity, there emerged for the first time practical men with a scientific bent, for whom the emergencies of the period became the cause of penetrating research. On their work rested the progress which in the middle of the eighteenth century

[1] Hasbach, with that incorrect scientific judgment which mars his work, otherwise so meritorious, has rated Sir James Stewart far too highly. When all is said, however, Stewart's work belongs to the greatest achievements in our field.

led to the definite establishment of our discipline in England. To these no less a man than Locke belonged (*Some Considerations of the Consequences of the Lowering of Interest and Raising the Value of Money*, 1695 and *Further Considerations*, 1696), in whom, if we disregard superficialities, the economist has completely replaced the philosopher.[1] He contributed much not only to the theory of money but also penetrated into the problem of value—from the point of view of the labour theory of value—and he offers in addition a rudimentary theory of distribution. Above all he went more deeply into the question on what particular factors the economic well-being of a nation depends. Confronting him there could be found as a worthy, partly even superior, adversary Nicholas Barber, *A Discourse of Trade*, 1690, ed. Hollander, 1905. (On Barber compare St Bauer in *Conrad's Jahrbuch*, 1890.) As an adversary of Locke he is of importance as an opponent of the legal theory of money which today rouses so much interest, and of the theory of the balance of trade, using arguments which in essence anticipate those of Hume. His importance, however, does not rest on this but on the manner in which he established his results. In order to arrive at an attitude in practical questions he went back, as far as possible, to the ultimate elements of the economic process. He approached his goal step by step, settling theoretically one element of the problem after the other, and he realized how necessary it was to gain a definite theoretical point of view based on principles before approaching individual groups of facts. In doing so he outlined a theory of value based on the factor of utility, which was elegantly analysed by him, even if he came somewhat to grief over his theory of price which he tried to base quite correctly on the former. In

[1] This is why we mention him here and not together with the 'philosophers'. On him Vanderlint, a Dutch merchant (*Money Answers All Things*, 1734), was based, whose ideas on economic policy—regarding free trade and others—seem to have had some literary success, although scientifically he is of little importance. The same applies to Asgill (*Several Assertions Proved*, 1694, ed. Hollander) and Berkeley's *Querist*. The Dutch writings of this epoch offer a considerable amount of interesting material and show roughly the same features as their English counterparts, though in the seventeenth century they were a shade more advanced. I cannot, however, deal with them but should like to mention Graswinckel (1600-68), Salmasius (1588-1658) and de la Court (1618-85).

his theory of interest he turned his back resolutely on the opinion, then held universally, that interest was paid for money, thus anticipating the analysis of capital, undertaken in the two subsequent centuries.[1] As regards the theory of interest, however, he was already surpassed by the treatise *The Interest of Money Mistaken, or a Treatise Proving that the Abatement of Interest is the Effect and not the Cause of the Riches of a Nation*, which appeared in 1668. Its great merit, which in our opinion represented a milestone on the way towards an understanding of the phenomenon of interest, is indicated in the subtitle. Of all the achievements of this period which are accessible to us today—this naturally depends partly merely on chance—only the book by Sir Dudley North, *Discourses Upon Trade*, 1691, ed. Hollander, 1907, is of a similar calibre. Already the preface is noteworthy, though it is stated in it that it was not written by the author himself, it shows, however, an unmistakable resemblance to the phraseology in the text.

In this book we find a realistic and scientific theory of economics, consciously contrasted with the 'ordinary and vulgar conceits being meer Husk and Rubbish', and a reference to modern methods of Natural Science. The whole train of thought, moreover, of these two treatises which present the earliest penetrating analysis in favour of free trade does honour to the methodological principles on which the argument is based. The author perceives clearly that it is merely the narrow outlook of the practical men of his era which accounts for the views then prevailing and he sets out to replace them by a discerning analysis of exceptional forcefulness. Not until the days of Ricardo did theoretical speculation surpass this masterpiece. The magnificent conception of all nations forming a community of trade, the clear realization that in the sense in which former writers had assumed it, harmful branches of trade did not exist, the idea that governmental regulation of prices is ineffective or injurious to everybody concerned, that the circulation of currency regulated itself automatically, if there was free-

[1] 'Interest is the rent of stock and is the same as the rent of land,' he says. If everything that a modern reader tries to read into this phrase really is contained in it this equation of capital- and land-rent represents an immense progress in analysis.

dom to mint money—all these points are found in his writings and establish his claim to glory in the field of economics. The significance of his work is in no way diminished by the numerous and necessary qualifications which had to be added at a later period. If we want to study the development of scientific thought in our field we cannot do better than to compare, say, Mun, North, Smith and Ricardo.

In the eighteenth century it was Hume who together with others—as e.g. Joseph Massie, *The Natural Rate of Interest*, 1750—continued these achievements. About his economic essays similar statements can be made as about the economic writings of Locke: his philosophy had a greater effect on other economists than it had on himself. In him we meet a man with a clear mind who has the measure of his time without being a profound thinker. It has become fashionable to praise him at the expense of Adam Smith; the discovery of a literary connection has led people to exaggerate its importance in this case just as much as in others. It is true that Hume played an eminent part in the progress which Economics made after it had flagged in the first half of the eighteenth century. Yet his brilliant analytical essays, *Essays, Moral and Political*, ed. Green and Groves, 1875—which, incidentally, were not the products of his creative period—merely administered the death-blow to moribund conceptions, and their effect was primarily of a popularizing nature. In details there are traces of carelessness and there is nowhere the grandeur of his philosophical work. Although nothing was produced in this period which is so readable and affords such insight into the growth of economics it is obvious that in our field the whole power of his genius did not make itself felt. Tucker (1712–1799, compare W. E. Clark, *Josiah Tucker*) produced more solid results; in his work the subject-matter of economics began as it were to settle down, but the palm must be awarded to Cantillon, whose essay *Essai sur la nature du commerce en général* was completed in 1734—it was originally written in English and reprinted in 1892—and can be considered as the first systematic attempt to work over the whole field of economics. Its author bears the stamp of the scientific spirit, the various problems dealt with by him appear as if they had been permeated by uniform principles and they form part of a complete analysis of grand design. The narrowness of former ways of thought has been overcome, primitive mistakes are avoided and there are just as many that must be attributed to lack of training in the art of analysis as those that are due to the influence of philosophy.[1]

The life work of Sir William Petty, *Taxes and Contributions*, 1662, *Political Arithmetic*, 1682, *Political Anatomy of Ireland*, 1691, stands somewhat apart from the development outlined above. He was particularly interested in comprehending economic problems in statistical terms. In this respect he differed from his contemporaries amongst whom this statistical approach to economics was quite usual merely by the wide range of his speculations; at that time this kind of undertaking was considered comparatively easy, which was only natural since its difficulties can be clearly seen only at a higher stage of development. While, however, Petty's contemporaries often regarded statistics merely as a means by which they could grasp phenomena quantitatively which otherwise did not appear to them particularly problematical, Petty tried to master the material theoretically and to interpret it purposefully in a way in which this had hardly been attempted before. He created for himself theoretical tools with which he tried to force a way through the undergrowth of facts, and in consequence we find theoretical considerations full of vigour and thoughtfulness at every step. As regards depth of economic knowledge the remaining representatives of 'Political Arithmetics' are clearly inferior to Petty, although some of them were epoch-making in other respects, especially Graunt, Davenant and Gregory King. The latter scored a success which found very few imitators but which secured for this reason all the more a kind of platonic approval: the establishment of King's law which represented an attempt to ascertain numerically the relation between price and the available supply of wheat. This

[1] In addition we may mention John Harris, whose treatise *On Money and Coins*, 1755, happily represents not merely the net result of English discussions on money but contains also the main features of a general theory of economics; also John Law (*Money and Trade Considered*, 1705), the well-known financier, whose work rises above a merely topical pamphlet because of his theory of credit, although it was devoted to the popularization of a plan to base paper money on land, often advanced at that period.

approval was well merited. King's achievement lay in a field which sooner or later had to be fully explored.

Taken as a whole, however, this very promising development petered out. Economic research for a long time to come pursued quite different paths and statistical research became separated from it. It is impossible to deal with other phenomena of this period more closely. We should merely like to emphasize the fact that it was also in the seventeenth century that comparative descriptions of the economic conditions in various countries made their first appearance—we may mention as an example Sir William Temple's *Observations on the Netherlands*, 1693—which formed a group by themselves, just as they do to a large extent still today. Success was also achieved in certain specialized fields, as regards for instance problems of poverty and unemployment, and this success was to dominate public opinion for a long time.[1]

Thus in England a picture of great vitality in our field reveals itself to us, the study of which is not only essential for an understanding of the growth of economics but also extremely attractive in itself. It is in the nature of things, however, that even in England all that was permanently valuable can be compressed into a small number of performances—approximately perhaps a dozen—but these were so to speak waves which emerged from a broad stream, while, as has already been mentioned, such a stream was absent on the Continent. In Germany the low level of economic literature reflected the devastations produced by the religious wars. Before this period, we find in the sixteenth century beginnings which enable us to assume that without these struggles and their political and social consequences a similar movement would have started in Germany as well. We find discussions on currency policy—amongst them the famous Albertine-Ernestine controversy of 1530—debates about the export of money, about the question of commercial companies, the problems of the peasants and others. The level of these discussions was not lower than was the case in England, but they did not develop and did not rise to the heights which in the normal course of events might have been expected. The consequence of this was the adoption of foreign achievements

[1] Compare Kostanecki, *Arbeit und Armut*, 1909.

which completely hampered an indigenous original development.

Even if the work of individual scholars suffered to a lesser extent it nevertheless lacked the fresh breath of air from the life of everyday economics. All knowledge, however, is the work of centuries and missing links in the chain of development are irreplaceable. It is possible to grasp logically conclusions that are offered by an outsider, but if such conclusions have not been produced in one's own country by former generations they will always be met with that lack of emotional understanding which will prevent the organic development of what has been taken over. This is the reason why economic theory could never take root as securely in Germany as it did in England and why its basic conceptions as a rule were received coolly and were met with that instinctive dislike which from the start favoured all kinds of objections and deviations from purely economic themes.

There were compensations, however. For no nation did the State and its organs become an object of such inexhaustible interest as it did for the Germans, and it dominated their intellectual life to a greater extent than happened anywhere else. Moreover, this peculiarity is of much greater importance than would appear at first glance. The German not only thought much more about the State than anybody else did but he understood something quite different by the term 'State'—to him it was the German territorial prince and his officials—his conceptions were also derived from quite different premises than those of Englishmen or Frenchmen. The nascent civil service state appeared to him not only as his most valuable national possession but altogether as the most essential factor in the progress of civilization, as well as an end in itself. Since as the result of the prevailing conditions almost nothing could be done in practical life without the civil service State it came finally about that all scientific reflection as well centred round the State.[1]

[1] There is a tendency in Germany to consider as a defect the prevalence of the opposite point of view dominant in England and expressed in Dr Johnson's couplet:

> How small of all that human hearts endure
> that part, that kings and laws can cause or cure.

The historical role of this point of view, however, must no more be misunderstood than the local and historical importance of the German en-

Administrative Law in Germany in a certain sense assumed the same role that economics played in England. If people concerned themselves with economics in England the result was a doctrine of social economy, while in Germany a doctrine of State economy resulted. Whereas in England within the group of writers of whom we are talking the merchant wrote for the merchant, in Germany the official wrote for the official. All this is of course valid only with those qualifications which we must always make in such a sketch which has to be confined to a few strokes of the pen. Without going into the matter more deeply we should like to stress the fact that these factors determined not only the manner in which this branch of the German science of the State was presented but also its guiding principles—the result was the science of cameralistics (*Kameralwissenschaft*).

This science is the doctrine of administration of a more or less absolutist territory. The interest of the territorial prince dominates the scene and is the centre round which the facts that lie within the ken of the various authors are being arranged. The investigation of these facts is to yield rules for the policy of the princes and the behaviour of the different organs of the State. From the beginning it is the total complex of all political tasks that is taken into account, while the individual problem is never an object of treatment for its own sake but only as part of the whole. In consequence, systematic treatment of the enormous subject matter appeared as the most important task, and this interest in a systematic approach has characterized economics in Germany to this day. Altogether, the training in public finance and the basic attitude of its teachers have made an essential contribution to the development of economics in Germany; even today its special character can largely be explained as the result of the preparatory work of the cameralists. Within the framework of the system arrived at, all attainable facts were carefully collated, partly for the benefit of the budding civil servant, partly also as a basis for discussions which, however, never went

thusiasm for the State. We must also add that it was of fundamental scientific importance to oppose the popular belief that the 'State' could do everything as if it were a superior power and to stress the objective causation of social events.

very far or very deeply.

Not only the basic attitude to the State but also the given foundations of social and political organization and even the essential principles of Politics were accepted without criticism and indeed without much analytical effort as self-evident and indisputable. The very fact, however, that the material was collected and ordered ensured that the 'art of government' went beyond mere empiricism. It provided the intellectual life-blood for the practice of administration and reflected and generalized every step in its progress. Thus one must not rate these spokesmen of the school of public finance as economists, not because they achieved nothing in this field, but because their main contribution was made elsewhere. The forerunners, as Osse (*Testament*, 1556), Loehneisen (*Aulico-politica*, 1622–24) and Obrecht (*Fünff unterschiedliche Secreta Politica von . . . guter Policey*, 1617), even the greatest original representative of the school of public finance, Seckendorf (*der teutsche Fürstenstaat*, 1678), offer us the judgments on topical economic problems of experienced and far-sighted men, not only without any attempts at deeper analysis but also without any lively interest in economic problems as such. When all is said, however, they were hardly below the general level of the time, in fact their characteristic approach makes them noticeably superior to the popular economists of other countries.

In a history of the theory of public finance it would be necessary to say something more, especially about Seckendorff; for our purposes, however, his in other respects far inferior contemporaries Becher (*Politischer Discurs von den eigentlichen Ursachen des Auf- und Abnehmens der Städte, Länder und Republicken*, 1668) and Hörnick (*Oesterreich über alles, was es nur will*, 1684), are of greater importance, since in these thinkers economic problems predominated. These two, however, do not really belong to the cameralistic school though they were strongly influenced by it. Hörnick's book is merely the description of a programme of commercial policy as understood at that period, whereas in Becher's book we find amongst a mass of valueless phrases genuine economic analyses, or at least attempts in this direction. He attempted to explain the problem of the effects of different forms of economic organization—monopoly, free competition (Polypol), and competition limited by privileges (Propol)—and to grasp the character and interaction of the various groups of economic professions. Yet only a much more detailed discussion of much more specialized questions would have led to really valuable results. This was precluded by the whole attitude towards economics which prevailed in this group.

Of the remaining Cameralists only Justi and Sonnenfels can be mentioned here. Neither of these two was really creative and both owe much to foreign influences in the economic field, yet in their work a great progress can be detected. Already their formal arrangement of the economic material differs completely from that of the older Cameralists. In the hands of Justi the science of administration *Polizei*[1], from which later the economic policy of Germany developed (*Polizeywissenschaft*, 1st ed. 1756), definitely constituted itself, though it was based entirely on the ideas of his predecessors in spite of all his criticism of the latter. As regards plan and aim the difference from the *Wealth of Nations* is by no means so immense as we should believe, while as regards clarity and insight the two works are separated by the labours of a century. Justi's arguments are valuable and ingenious merely in the field of the technique of administration; in economic matters he completely lacked training and mastery of the various approaches which were already at the disposal of his time. In this connection we are not thinking of the practical measures which he recommended. These practical judgments indeed almost always revealed sound common sense, yet this does not alter the fact that the fundamental structure of his analysis was inferior. The same cannot be said of Sonnenfels (*Grundsätze der Polizey, Handlung und Finanz*, 1765), who possessed such a fundamental structure and who above all mastered the economic theory which prevailed prior to Adam Smith. (Though he later quoted Adam Smith himself he revealed no understanding for the importance of his work.) His influence continued until well into the nineteenth century, although he was by no means an original thinker. He assimilated foreign influences with an open mind

[1] Translator's footnote. 'Polizei' at that time denoted much more than 'police'; it really meant administration in the widest sense.

and happily adapted them to German needs, recognizing with unfailing vision what was viable in them, but he created nothing new himself.

It is remarkable how meagre the literature of France was before the Physiocrats appeared upon the scene. It would almost appear as if the Government which in France also limited the chances of the development of economic discussions by depriving them of their practical purpose did not have the will to do things as well as possible and to train for this purpose a staff of teachers as Prussia had done in particular. There were lively enough discussions in other fields, but the circles that were most representative of intellectual life were not at all interested in questions of economics, or merely in a superficial fashion. Boisguillebert, who was not particularly rich in ideas and who could be compared with Petty, stood quite by himself. His *Dissertation sur la nature des richesses* (published in the last years of the seventeenth century or in the first of the eighteenth; it was much more important than his often quoted *Détail de France*, published first in 1695, and his *Fortune de France*, 1707) and other smaller works contained sensible criticism of many mistaken conceptions of the period which he, however, represented in as unfavourable an interpretation as possible. Yet it is absurd to turn him into a precursor of the Physiocrats, as there is nothing in him of those elements that constitute the character of the latter. It is moreover possible to quote Melon (*Essai politique sur le commerce*, 1734) and Dutot *Réflêxions politiques sur les finances et sur le commerce* as writers on economics, while with the best will in the world it would be impossible to consider Vauban, St Pierre, Fénélon and others either as scientific economists or as precursors of such. They discussed, clearly and intelligently, social and political problems. Many people did so at that time, and the existence of dictionaries alone (e.g. the *Dictionnaire du commerce* by the brothers Savary) proves that in these discussions economic problems were not forgotten. In the work of analysis, however, no progress was made.

In Italy there existed at first a literature which was quite parallel to the German cameralist school and in fact influenced the latter. We find very few economic arguments either in Carafa (*De regis et boni principis officio*) or in the sixteenth century in the writings of Palmieri, Botero or Machiavelli. Branches of this school still flourished in the nineteenth century but they need not be considered in an account of the development of economic knowledge. In addition we find similar current problems and controversies as in England and Germany—besides the question of protective agrarian tariffs which at that time was nowhere else of practical importance—all these produced economic researches. On two occasions these researches rose to the level of performances of the first rank, and here Italy produced the best effort which that period had to offer in this field. First of all this was true in the sphere of currency problems. Here it would be possible to name quite a few authors, but we will limit ourselves to achievements of a purely scientific character of the first order. The sixteenth century produced the work of Scaruffi (1579) and Davanzati (1588), the seventeenth century the work of Montanari (1680 and 1683), and the eighteenth century that of Galiani. Davanzati's dissertation is an immortal masterpiece of a clear and unfailingly penetrating analysis which illuminates all individual phenomena in the light of a basic principle of interpretation. He developed a 'metallic' theory of money based on a general conception of value in use which could be maintained even today. Galiani's work (1750) likewise can partly be read like a modern text book. It already embodies the main achievements in this field and it is only in quite modern times that the theory of money has substantially surpassed these labours. What lifts these works high above even many achievements of the nineteenth century is in particular the way in which they go right back to the elements of economic life in order to apply the principles arrived at to the theory of money.

Secondly, it was the commercial policy of the period which blossomed out into some first-class literary efforts, even though the accomplishments in this field cannot be compared with those mentioned just now. As in England it was the popular demand for a regulation of the rates of exchange by the State that set things moving in Italy as well. It was to the credit of Antonio Serra (*Breve trattato delle cause che possono far abbondare li regni d'oro et d'argento dove non sono miniere*), 1613, to have shown that the rates of exchange essentially reflected the balance account and to have added some profound discussions of the causes which determine the latter as well as of the chances of influencing it in turn. He is very considerably superior to Mun if by nothing else than by his entire manner of approach which is a genuinely scientific one. It must be admitted, however, that his whole examination of the problem how in a country without mines an abundance of gold and silver could be produced, was extremely primitive. Nobody can be blamed, however, for having taken over the problems of his age in the way in which they were offered to him. The solution was better than the method of questioning and Serras found many adherents. Amongst his successors Belloni (1750) and above all Genovesi (1765) are worth mentioning. The latter was a very independent thinker who is usually referred to as one of the precursors of the subjective theory of value. He was chiefly important, however, because he tried to formulate a systematic theory of economic life.

The authors mentioned above have many basic features in common. They and many others, whom we cannot name here, in a certain sense formed a group of their own. Apart from them—and apart also from the labours of the Venetian circle (Zanon, Arduino, Canciani)—there stood G. Ortes, although he was a Venetian by birth. His main work was: *Economica nazionale*, 1744. This work, which incidentally reminds us in many ways of Sir James Steuart,[1] with its grandiose attempt at a synthesis belongs to that large group of writings the authors of which have almost a claim to the title of a 'founder' of our discipline. The day for our science had come, all elements for its establishment had been given and what remained to be done now was to formulate successfully and vigorously what was in the air. There were many who felt this and who undertook

[1] The parallels between the two authors in the arrangement of their works and in many details are unmistakable and extremely interesting. Nothing is farther from our mind than the desire to search for plagiarism, but the fact of the parallelism itself in view of the absence of external relations is very remarkable and instructive. There can be no doubt that Ortes, who had stayed in England, was partly under English influence, but this of course proves nothing except that similar causes in similar circumstances produce similar consequences.

the attempt. Indeed, nothing would be more instructive than a survey of these attempts and of the causes of their failure, but it is not possible for us to go into this question more deeply. We may merely stress the fact that Ortes tried as it were to arrive at an economic sociology and that we find in his writings many weapons from the armoury of later economists. (The law of diminishing returns, the Malthusian principle of population and others.[1]) The Italian economic theory accordingly could hold its own next to that of England, but towards the end of the eighteenth century a decline set in and for a long time the Italian theory stood under foreign influence.

We have avoided so far mentioning even the word 'Mercantilism'. In fact, this term does not belong to a history of our subject. Indeed, almost all the writings quoted by us reflect the struggle of economic systems for authority and supremacy, and writers as well as politicians of this period took it for granted that national commercial policy should serve national ends. This latter view they did not discuss at all, it was discussed only by their opponents who were at first isolated, but later became more numerous and finally predominated. Yet Mercantilism was neither a scientific school nor a scientific theory—there were then no schools at all in our sense of the word—and we distort the picture if we seek already in this period what was in fact the consequence of a specialized discipline after it had properly constituted itself. Its importance for analysis in the field of social science fell short of its importance as a means for the creation of national economic units. We can be interested only in one question: What was the value for the progress of economics of those works that were occasioned by this 'system' of economic policy? It has indeed become a truism today to say that the criticism of the immediately following period was unjust, though the argument that the practical proposals of the mercantilist writers were justified by the conditions that prevailed at that time does not carry any weight with us. For their scientific

[1] In his *Riflessioni sulla popolazione*, 1790. Compare also Lampertico, *G. Ortes*, 1865. Loria, *La modernita di G. Ortes Atti dell' istituto Veneto*, 1900-1, Vol. 60. Arias, 'La teorica di disoccupazino di G. Ortes,' *Giornale degli Econ.*, 1908. There can be no question of a special method, such as some scholars ascribe to Ortes.

attempts this argument is not entirely valid in any case. Yet there are other considerations which make the mercantilist writers appear in a more favourable light to us. First of all they were entirely misinterpreted. The charge that they identified wealth with the possession of gold and silver, levelled against them on numerous occasions, loses some of its validity if in those passages which could be quoted in support of this charge we replace the term 'wealth' by that of index of wealth.[1] This can be done the more easily since it could not possibly have occurred to them to see in the acquisition of precious metals the final aim of economic life and since in fact the identification referred to above merely represented a definition which in itself was of little importance. It must be added that the entire monetary policy of this age offered in point of fact so much cause for reflection that it was indeed possible to see in its discussion the noblest task of the economic theory of the period altogether.

Further, in judging this branch of our subject and more particularly its mercantilist highlights, we must always bear in mind that they were the first in the field. From this point of view much for which they were blamed in fact redounds to their credit. This is especially true of their theory of the balance of trade; before we discuss whether they overestimated its importance or not we should indeed recognize that its discovery and formulation constituted a great achievement—as a matter of fact it was the first step towards an analysis of economic factors. Incidentally, it is entirely wrong to assume that later protectionists compare all that favourably with the Mercantilists. By far the majority of later arguments, if not all of them, could be met in their writings already, a fact which we cannot elaborate here, and it was only the knowledge of the objections and altogether the better training resulting from our discipline having fully matured in the meantime, that distinguish most later writers from their predecessors, whom, however,

[1] These passages, besides, are much less frequent than the early critics of mercantilism give us to understand. When this was discovered it became at first necessary to distinguish between strictly orthodox mercantilists and less hardened sinners amongst them. In this process the former group became less and less numerous, the more closely one looked, and a reaction in favour of the whole 'school' set in long ago.

they almost always disowned. In connection with this another achievement emerged: The lucid definition of national interests as distinguished from private ones and the recognition of the possibility of a clash between the two. No doubt, the Mercantilists over-estimated this possibility, but whatever we may think about this it is certain that the real or apparent proof for the harmony of all social and private interests was possible only on the basis of the preparatory work done by the Mercantilists. They did not recognize the nature of the circular flow of economic life, even less did they have a correct idea of the interaction of the various spheres of individual economies within the framework of the national economy. The phenomenon of the national economy itself, however, was as it were discovered by them and conceived as something independent and real.

II

THE DISCOVERY OF THE CIRCULAR FLOW OF ECONOMIC LIFE

THE PHYSIOCRATS.[1] (ADAM SMITH)

1. We have seen that our science like all others originated in individual researches into striking facts which appeared as problems even to the layman. As long as men confined themselves to such research and as long as the central phenomenon of economics itself remained more or less in the darkness of instinctive and practical knowledge, scientific analysis could never fully set to work, it could not, as it were, make full use of its vital powers. It was impossible to build up a basic stock of knowledge of principles, nor could a staff of expert workers really form itself. It was necessary to derive an explanatory principle from each separate complex of facts—as it were in a gigantic struggle with them—and it was at best possible merely to sense the great general contexts, an understanding of which is essential—even from a practical point

[1] Apart from the general literature on the history of economic doctrine, in which the physiocratic system is always being dealt with (especially by Oncken and Denis) we may mention the following: Oncken, article on Quesnay in *Handwörterbuch der Staatswissenschaften.* Lexis, article on Physiocrats, *ibidem*, also *Entstehen und Werden der physiokratischen Theorie*, Frank. Vierteljahrsschrift, 1896-7. Güntzberg, *Gesellschafts- und Staatslehre der Physiokraten*, 1907. Higgs, *The Physiocrats*, 1897. Hasbach, *Die Allgemeinen philosophischen Grundlagen der von F. Quesnay und A. Smith begründeten Volkswirtschaftslehre*, 1870. Schelle, *Dupont de Nemours et l'école physiocratique*, 1888. Lavergne, *Les économistes du XVIIIe siècle.* Weulersee, *Le mouvement physiocratique*, 1910. St Bauer, *Zur Enstehung der Physiokratie*, Conrad's *Jahrbücher*, 1890. Seligman, 'Some Neglected British Economists', *Econ. Journal* XIII. Picard, *Etude sur quelques theories du salaire au XVIIIe siècle, Revue d'histoire des doctrines écon.*, 1910. Pervinquiere, *Contribution à l'etude de la productivité dans la physiocratie*, Ph.D. thesis. Labriola, *Doctrine economiche di F. Quesnay*, 1897. In addition to the edition of the physiocratic works by Guillaumin we have at present the edition by Geuthner.

of view—for the explanation of the more subtle effects and counter-effects of economic phenomena. It is these general contexts which science can add to the knowledge of a clear-minded and well-informed practical man. In all the best minds in our field we have seen established a tendency to bring to light these general contexts, to make their investigation their main concern and to treat the conclusions emerging from such an investigation as the main part of economics. It was, however, the Physiocrats or 'Economists' who made the great breach, through which lay all further progress in the field of analysis, by the discovery and intellectual formulation of the circular flow of economic life. This is not to say that the fact itself in its popular meaning—the periodical sowing and harvesting for instance—could ever have been unknown, but here we are concerned with the economic sense and the economic formulation of the phenomenon: the task was to ascertain how each economic period becomes the basis for the subsequent one, not only in a technical sense but also in the sense that it produces exactly such results as induce and enable the members of the economic community to repeat the same process in the same form in the next economic period; how economic production comes about as a social process, how it determines the consumption of every individual and how the latter in its turn determines further production, how every act of production and consumption influences all other acts of production and consumption, and how, as it were, every element of economic energy completes a definite route year in year out under the influence of definite motive forces. Only with the help of such an analysis was it possible for further knowledge of the economic life process of society to develop and were scholars enabled to survey all the general factors and their functions as well as all the elements which have to be considered in every individual problem as far as it is purely economic. As long as economic periods were viewed merely as a technical phenomenon, and the fact of the economic cycle through which they move had not been recognized, the connecting link of economic causality and an insight into the inner necessities and the general character of economics were missing. It was possible to consider the individual acts of exchange, the phenomenon of money, the question of protective tariffs as economic problems, but it was impossible to view with clarity the total process which unfolds itself in a particular economic period. Before the Physiocrats appeared on the scene only local symptoms on the economic body, as it were, had been perceived, while they enabled us to conceive this body physiologically and anatomically as an organism with a uniform life process and uniform conditions of life, and it was they who presented to us the first analysis of this life process. On this point only platitudes had existed before them, they were the first to direct their attention to the inner workings of the social exchange of goods and the phenomenon of their constant self-renewal.

It is no mere accident that they formed at the same time the first genuine economic 'school', since only a total conception could form the basis for one. The historian of economic thought is rarely in a position to name the founder of a school with such certainty as he can do in this case. All essential ideas and at the same time all the vigour of an outstanding personality were combined in François Quesnay, who had created these ideas from within himself to a far greater degree than any other economist had done. He was one of the greatest and most original thinkers in our field. Those who joined him were or became his pupils and subordinated themselves to him in a way for which we have no other example in our field. Only the most important names and works may be mentioned: Quesnay himself (1694-1774) exercised above all a personal influence. Of his scattered publications (edited by Oncken in 1888) we should like to mention only his *Droit naturel* (1765), which contains his sociology and his *Tableau économique* (1758), which contains a systematic presentation of his basic conceptions. Clearly bearing in mind the state of affairs in our field at about 1750 we realize that we feel ourselves nowhere else in economic literature so near to creative genius as when we regard the conception of this work alone which, as Madame Pompadour correctly predicted, would appear to most critics at best as a harmless intellectual toy.

The zeal of the disciples tried to counteract the complete lack of understanding with which the 'Tableau' was met. Above all we must mention here Le Trosne (*De l'ordre social*, 1777), Baudeau (*Première introduction à la philosophie économique*, 1771), in the third place Lemercier de la Rivière (*L'ordre naturel et essential des sociétés politiques*, 1767), finally, Dupont de Nemours (*Physiocratie ou constitution naturelle du gouvernement le plus avantaguex au genre humain*, 1767). The elder Mirabeau, who, after Quesnay's death, was regarded as the head of the small group, had already created for himself a well defined system of ideas without the help of Quesnay—but probably not without that of Cantillon (*L'ami des hommes*, first part, 1763). It was only later that he became dependent on Quesnay (continuations of *L'ami des hommes*, *Philosophie moral ou économie generale et politique de l'agriculture*, 1763), but because of this never quite so completely as did the others. Turgot (*Réfléxions sur la formation et la distribution des richesses*, published in 1769, *Sur les prêts d'argent*, 1769, *Valeurs et monnaies*, *Lettres sur la liberté du commerce des grains*, 1770, and others) was very close to the group without actually belonging to it. The Physiocrats did not meet with genuine understanding or with adversaries worthy of them. The controversy with Forbonnais[1] was barren and just as superficial as Voltaire's mockery in his *Homme aux quarante écus*. Galiani, whom we have met already in his *Dialogues* (1770), did not approach the problem fundamentally, just as the whole controversy about the corn duties, the temporary abolition of which was much debated in France, did not bear much theoretical fruit. Condillac (*Le commerce et le gouvernement*, 1776) deserves mention not because of his criticism of the Physiocrats but because of his positive achievements. Mably (*Doutes proposés aux philosophes économiques*, 1768, essentially a critical review of Lemercier) cannot be rated as an economist, and Morellet is of importance merely as a man dealing with practical problems.[2]

Most supporters of the Physiocrats grasped the inner meaning of their doctrines as little as did their enemies. Amongst the Ger-

[1] Compare Oncken in his *Geschichte der Nationalökonomie*. Forbonnais' main work is *Principes Economiques*, 1767.

[2] The Swiss writer Herrenschwand was no physiocrat but an able disciple of theirs (*De l'économie politique moderne*, 1786; *De l'économie politique et morale de l'espèce humaine*, 1786; *Du vrai principe actif de l'économie politique*, 1797); compare about him A. Jöhr, *Herrenschwand*, 1901.

mans pride of place belongs to Margrave Carl Friedrich von Baden Durloch (*Abrégé des principes de l'économie politique*, 1786) and to Mauvillon (*Physiokratische Briefe an Professor Dohm*), 1780; others like Schlettwein, Schmalz (died 1831), Krug (died 1843) and the Swiss Iselin merely kept to superficialities. Matters were similar in Italy where Neri, Beccaria, Filangieri, Verri and others appropriated one or the other statement to which they had taken a fancy. In England, too, there is a small number of physiocratic writings. More important than these, however, is the influence which the Physiocrats exercised on Adam Smith and on a group of later writers, amongst whom was Karl Marx. It was precisely the originality of their system which prevented them from becoming immediately and widely effective. Their firm conviction by its very obstinacy obtained respect and praise, but on looking more closely we find that their great momentary success with Parisian society did not mean very much. All novel theoretical thought is at first always absorbed in a merely superficial sense which in most cases has nothing in common with its true significance. Many readers naïvely saw in the matter simply a glorification of agriculture, and all those to whom this appealed declared themselves as supporters of the system. It is impossible to give here a more detailed account of what happened to the Physiocrats and their writings.

2. The physiocratic doctrine, as has already been stated, is a branch of the large family of systems of Natural Law and must be approached in very much the same way as the latter. It intended to be not merely an economic theory but also a general sociology which consisted, however, of economic material and which placed economic considerations into the foreground. Nevertheless we propose to limit ourselves to the economic theory proper as it was outlined by the Physiocrats. This obviously was an analytical achievement: the Physiocrats sought to comprehend intellectually the general character of the economic process on the basis of generally known facts of experience without considering it necessary to carry out a systematic collection of individual facts. Denis called their method an inductive one, at any rate it was theoretical in exactly the same sense as it was for instance in the case of

Ricardo. This is quite clear, but in the case of the Physiocrats as with all teachers of Natural Law there was superimposed the idea that a definite and concrete economic order and a definite behaviour in practical questions of economic policy corresponded to the economic essence of the matter. This order which was always before their eyes and which once and for all had to be considered as ideal and in support of which they sought to adduce every possible sanction, even a divine one, is their *ordre naturel.* This in fact gives the whole system an unscientific finalist character. If the Physiocrats employed metaphysical statements or any practical postulates within their analytical system of thought and if they based their results on them their doctrine would in consequence lose its scientific character, but this is not the case. The nucleus of their argumentation is entirely free from such elements, as we can easily convince ourselves if we use the decisive criterion of omitting the statements concerned and of replacing the finalist construction of some other statements by a causal one. Thus it is possible to separate their scientific analysis of the facts from the statement of their opinion that the result of this analysis is at the same time the best possible concrete order of things under a divine plan.[1] Once we have realized this and have recognized that their statements are based directly on their examination of fundamental economic facts, it becomes senseless to search for theological or philosophic determining causes. The moment when Quesnay for instance in examining the nature of capital says to us: 'Parcourez les fermes et ateliers et voyez . . .' etc. (*Dialogue sur le commerce*, edited by Daire, 1846), he vindicated the scientific character of his argumentation. Whether in so doing he was a Deist or not, whether a Free Trader or not, whether bureaucratic absolutism or self-government pleased him more—all this was very important to him, so important in fact that Turgot could declare he was no Physiocrat 'because he much rather had no king', it is moreover

[1] Gide has spoken, as did Denis, of the theological character of the physiocratic system and used this to explain their theory—an example of the tendency of so many economists to cling to superficialities and of the predilection for the 'Philosophy' of economics. This becomes even more marked in Hasbach: this confusion of two completely different approaches makes it impossible to do justice to the scientific content of a system.

actually the main point for any history of contemporary thought, but for our purposes it is irrelevant and does not affect Quesnay's scientific importance one way or the other. Nevertheless, it was to his credit that he made an analysis of facts the main point, while his contemporaries, e.g. even Steuart, were mainly concerned with giving practical advice to the statesman.

The Physiocrats were in practice well aware of the analytical method, even if they did not see in their doctrine merely an intellectual re-creation of real events—as the classical writers were to do already. They believed that this intellectual re-creation expressed in sharply defined terms, which were free from other elements, certain basic patterns of the facts. In addition, however, they saw in their doctrine also an ideal picture in a practical sense. In this context we must not forget that this juxtaposition of different elements occurs much more frequently in the early stages of scientific effort than later, especially since the Physiocrats lacked the conception of social progress, so that the theoretical picture of reality could be considered as immutable and could, in consequence, become an absolute ideal and an element of a divine world order much more easily than could have happened if they had been conscious of the changeability of social facts. The Physiocrats created, if we may be allowed to express it in this way, a doctrine of the economic nature of the matter, of the factual causes of economic life. Yet it is impossible to talk in any other sense of a natural doctrine of the Physiocrats, certainly not in the sense that they, mistaking the peculair character of the social sphere, made the amateurish attempt to force upon it a conception which was derived from natural science and which gave the wrong impression of exactness. Their theory is merely an attempt to think systematically about that store of general knowledge which every practical man accumulates and which he uses as the basis of his behaviour, moreover, they tried to weld it into a uniform and consistent whole. To point out superficial resemblances or to stress the fact that scientific training could be acquired—at least at this period—only in the field of natural science is no proof to the contrary. In order to prove an illegitimate influence from the field of natural science it would be necessary to show in every particular instance, in every theoretical proposition, that they could be explained not by the arguments of an economic character, which had been or could be adduced in their support, but owed their existence to an artificial parallelism between natural science and the science of the mind (*Geisteswissenschaft*).

It is true that the Physiocrats continued the practice, established in the seventeenth century, of speaking of natural laws of economics and of the whole of social life. In order to understand the importance of this custom it is necessary to distinguish two points: Firstly, what they themselves meant by it consciously and, secondly, what we, after a century and a half, must see in these laws as regards their concrete content. As far as the first point is concerned we cannot expect the Physiocrats to have taken up a position which we could accept, since this question has remained controversial to this day. In the first place their conception of law was influenced by their finalism. They proceeded from the belief that the will of Providence is bound to reveal itself to the researching mind in the analysis of facts. Therefore, they saw in laws not merely rules applied to facts but something that stands outside the facts and to which man must subordinate himself. These laws implied commandments for human action and a system of duties. Besides, the Physiocrats showed no understanding for the difference between social and scientific laws of nature. Indeed the latter appeared to them—as they did to Newton—under exactly the same point of view.[1] In the second place we shall see that the so-called laws of the Physiocrats are exactly what we describe today as such without being contradicted, just because neither the theological nor

[1] For the term 'Law of Nature' does not necessarily as such mean a 'physical' law of nature, indeed, it is completely compatible with a recognition of the particular characteristics of the field of social science, a fact which is often overlooked. Even if, however, an author says expressly that the social and physical laws are essentially the same, we have to inquire in which sense this is meant. Even if, finally, it is meant in quite an untenable sense, justice demands an investigation whether merely this statement and the opinion of the author regarding the nature of his conclusions is erroneous—in which case there is very little cause for special blame and the results themselves are not affected—or whether the author allowed himself to be influenced materially by the naturalist error. Then, it is true, but only then, his conclusions fall to the ground, as far as their content is concerned.

the naturalist element was really the point from which they started. They merely expressed the results of economic analysis in this theological or naturalist form *after* they had established them. In view of their great achievement to have recognized definitely that economic life is subject to certain necessary factors which can be comprehended in their general character, and that in this field also causes have their effects, we must not judge too severely the numerous shortcomings of this diagnosis. Besides, even then, Montesquieu (1749) on one side and Turgot on the other arrived already at more perfect formulations.[1] Moreover, we may mention the fact that this period was already familiar with methodological controversies. Many opponents of the Physiocrats fought against their method as 'unrealistic' and too 'absolute', and it was Galiani in particular who in his dialogues pointed out how inadmissible general rules were for economic policy. This, it is true, did not invalidate the theory of the Physiocrats, but Galiani rejected the theory together with its practical consequences which seemed offensive to him and which seemed to follow inevitably from it. This practice became customary later on and has been continued until modern times. Turgot's attitude, too, which often almost amounted to dislike, can partly be explained by his view that the Physiocrats established general laws where there were none and thus did violence to the multiformity of life. Naturally, this attitude did not turn either Galiani or Turgot into representatives of a strictly historical relativism, since both of them did essentially theoretical work; but they occupied an intermediate position.

3. The Physiocrats approached their great task of presenting the general forms of the economic cycle merely with the already existing resources without adding anything themselves. They wished to combine the facts of economic needs with the general facts of the environment and to establish laws that could be applied to economic events. Their psychology was strictly individualist, rationalist and extremely simple. It can be summed up in the assumption of a desire for the greatest possible satisfaction of

[1] Montesquieu's formulation: 'Rapports necessaires qui derivent de la nature des choses' breathes completely the modern spirit. Gournay also must be mentioned here.

individual needs with the smallest possible exertion. In consequence the economic principle as formulated consciously and clearly by Quesnay formed their point of departure.[1] Their sociology likewise was simple. They accepted the social organization as they saw it before their eyes, partly as a matter of course, partly as sufficiently typical. It has already been mentioned that such procedure was to be expected in the early stages. We must further add that the over-estimation of actions that were in accordance with Reason and the incompleteness of a psychological analysis, as well as that atomistic approach which saw in the—essentially unchangeable—individual the key to all social happenings was least harmful in economic investigations. Although these factors make it impossible for people to see beyond a certain point and must lead in many respects to a caricature of reality as well, just for the formulation of a 'logic of economic facts', that is to say precisely for that achievement of the Physiocrats which concerns us most, they represent in part necessary and useful assumptions. We must, however, not try and build upon them alone a theory of the life process of society, a sociology. For their sociology and also for their practical insight into reality all these ideas were fatal, however much they talked of the 'homme social' and the 'vie collective' while their contributions to basic problems of economics was not thereby invalidated.[2]

In this field their achievements were great. Ungenerous and un-

[1] Obtenir la plus grande augmentation possible de jouissance par la plus grande diminution possible de dépenses.

[2] In such cases we must always ask: Firstly, is such a basic conception in itself and generally 'correct'? If this is denied our critical labours are by no means finished, but the further question arises: is the basic conception under review perhaps useful as a hypothesis? Does it not in the first place emphasize a real element, which being looked at in isolation, is of interest? And, furthermore, even if this is not the case, we must ask whether the deviation produced by the basic conception in question is considerable or whether there are circumstances which limit its significance. As regards the rationalist hypothesis, for instance, such a circumstance is found in the fact that certain necessary objective causes assert themselves and determine human actions even if the latter are not based on a rational insight or on clear motives. Or is it possible to formulate the objectionable statement in a better way? Critics are usually little worried by such questions, but any criticism which does not answer them is valueless.

appreciative criticism has for a long time prevented a just estimate of their performance and obscured the fact that all subsequent work was based on theirs. Moreover, certain peculiarities which stood out grotesquely have been emphasized again as if they constituted the essential points of the physiocratic doctrine, the refutation of which ended the matter. Adam Smith already started with this and only recently have we penetrated more deeply into the economic system of thought of the Physiocrats.

The total survey of the economic process which the Physiocrats achieved, the 'economic point of view' which they adopted, even though they started from the individual on the one side and from the natural 'milieu' on the other, is clearly expressed in three conceptions which assumed the greatest importance for economics: the conceptions of circulation, of the social product and that of its 'distribution'. The first was known already to popular discussions and to the Mercantilists, but it was merely the surface phenomenon of the circulation of money that had been thought of. Quesnay and his followers were the first to push aside the 'monetary veil' energetically, and a circulation of a different kind was revealed to them: They showed how during every economic period a quantity of commodities newly enters into the economy—in their way of thinking from the inexhaustible treasure of Nature—and is taken over and passed on to the final stage of consumption by the various groups of members of the economy. These groups are characterized by special functions, and the process of passing on the commodities is effected by exchange. Acts of exchange form the links in the chain which connects these groups or classes. Thus the economic life of a nation presents itself as a system of exchange relations which, renewing themselves periodically, fill the space between production and consumption. The quantity of goods produced during the economic period within the economic system is regarded as a social product which is being distributed every time.

This idea is so familiar to us today that we no longer regard it as striking, but it contained a bold abstraction and an innovation which was methodologically most important. This social product does not exist as such anywhere in reality, and is in itself an artificial intellectual creation. Yet it was the creation of this theoretical sum total which for the first time made possible, or at least facilitated, a deeper comprehension of the co-operation between the individual economies and of their mutual dependence. Moreover, the identification on principle of the social product with the wealth of the nation—the emphasis given to the point of view of the periodical circulation of commodities—gave to the conception of national wealth a precision which had been lacking before. In fact it clearly illuminated the relation between national wealth and production once and for all. These foundations have been preserved to this day and have proved themselves useful, as can be seen e.g. in the doctrine of A. Marshall.[1]

4. This is the framework within which the wealth of the nation (richesse) develops and has its being. Cantillon had shown remarkable insight when he wrote: 'La richesse en elle-même n'est autre chose que la nourriture, les commodités et les agréments de la vie', in his *Essai sur le commerce en général*, 1753, p. 1. The Physiocrats certainly did not improve on this statement when they defined wealth as the sum total of the economic goods produced yearly ('biens commerçables', Quesnay, *Oevres*, ed. by Oncken). We know already its motive force and its explanatory principle: 'le desire de jouir' according to an expression used by Lemercier. Thus we only have to stress one other essential factor: the physiocratic theory of the nature and function of capital. Before them a precise theory of capital had not existed, not only because mercantilist errors stand in the way of such a theory but also because before them the basic economic factors as such had not at all been analysed in detail. Such an analysis, however, is necessary for a precise conception of the part played by capital in the economic life of the nation in opposition to its importance for the individual economy, recognized in everyday life. Quesnay—and with him his true disciples—saw the function of capital in the necessity to maintain the worker during the period of production, in the *avances foncères*—the expenses for the clearing of the ground for cultivation—

[1] Philippovich (*Grundriss*, 1, book 4) has pointed out how unrealistic the conception of 'distribution' is and has replaced it by that of the formation of income which in fact has much to recommend itself. Yet this does not alter the historical importance and the usefulness of the presentation of the idea of distribution.

and in the *avances annuelles*—or better *fonds des avances* which are partly embodied in the produced means of production. The *avances annuelles* reproduce themselves yearly together with the interests on the *avances primitives*.[1] The substance of capital, therefore, is represented as that part of the social product of preceding economic periods which maintains the production of the current period—of temporarily particular importance as part of the circulation of commodities.

The development as conceived by the Physiocrats can best be expressed in the words of the Margrave of Baden, *Abrégé*, 1786, p. 7: The cyclical movement of labour and expense is made more perfect by more efficient labour. The latter increases the means of subsistence, the increase of which leads to an increase of the *espèce humaine*, which in turn increases the needs of the community and consequently the *dépenses*. Thus economic civilization develops from a primitive state of search for food (*l'homme vivoit des fruits épars et spontanés de la terre*) in which it was just this search for food which constituted labour, corresponding to the *dépenses de la subsistence* and representing the performance which procured the subsistence. In this context the Physiocrats naturally talked of 'duty' and 'right', but while they used language of the Law of Nature they meant exactly what we just expressed.

It is now, however, appropriate to deal more closely with those characteristics of the physiocratic system which in the history of economic doctrine have always been wrongly placed into the foreground. These characteristics did not effect the essence of the basic ideas outlined above and represented merely a somewhat premature attempt at elaborating them in a certain direction, but nevertheless for the Physiocrats themselves and for the fate of their theory they were of great importance. Once we have established these fundamental conceptions and are now looking for a firm point in the economic cycle, it is possible for our attention to be directed to the technical origin of the circular flow of economic life. We notice that in every economic period a certain quantity

[1] We must add the *avances primitives* themselves, *le bloc des richesses mobiliaires qui aident l'homme à la cultivation.* The *avances souveraines* are the expenses of the State on road construction, etc.

of materials enters into the social world from the lap of Nature on which directly or indirectly the whole community must live. It is this quantity which in a certain sense in fact circulates in a community and the periodical replacement of which enables us to distinguish the economic periods from each other. This point of departure was in itself an obvious one, it was bound to be specially familiar to Quesnay because of the analogy to the nutritional process of organic bodies. It is entirely superfluous to seek for any metaphysical reasons why the Physiocrats should have seized upon it, as if it represented an otherwise quite inexplicable aberration. It simply constituted the observation of a completely undeniable 'physical' fact—'Intérêt Social', as Le Trosne called it.

The Physiocrats admittedly became obsessed with this idea, once they had conceived it and they overrated its importance considerably. If we, however, think it out consistently and remember that it was merely formulated in order to explain the facts under observation, we realize that it became quite natural to confine the conception of production to that of original production, or, more strictly speaking, to that of the production of materials which could be repeated yearly *ad infinitum*—which meant that mining was excluded. It was, therefore, a matter of course that all labour not used for this original production was called unproductive. This did not constitute a special thesis but merely an analytical proposition in Kant's sense, the proposition: Labour not employed for original production does not produce new original products. The necessity and usefulness of such labour was not denied. If Le Trosne wrote: 'Le travail porté partout ailleurs que sur la terre, est stérile absolument, car l'homme n'est pas créateur,' he simply meant that human labour cannot create new matter, which as far as economics is concerned is only relevant if the conclusion is drawn which is implicit in the definition. If we want to see a special proposition in the statement quoted above it could merely be considered as correct.

The Physiocrats, however, on the one hand based too much on it and on the other, under the spell of their conception, closed their eyes to other more rewarding vistas. It redounded in the first place to their credit that they comprehended, with the help of theoretical principles, different classes as groups with special social interests and investigated their interaction, instead of merely empirically distinguishing them according to their different social functions, as had been done already previously. This achievement, together with the methodological conception of 'distribution', remained indeed a κτῆμα εἰς ἀεί of economics. It was unfortunate, however, that the Physiocrats applied these correct efforts to that factor which later analysis proved to be of secondary importance. The productive class, e.g. those participants in the economic process who apply labour and capital to production in the physiocratic sense retain for themselves part of the produce, of which in turn they pass a part to the sterile (industrial, etc.) class. The latter adds value to the product by their manufacture, but does so merely to the extent to which its members themselves consume; in consequence, they do not really produce value. The productive class passes this part of the produce to the sterile class by exchanging food and raw materials for industrial products. Since the latter, however, contain food and raw materials from former exchanges, and that to exactly the same amount, the value which had been passed on returns to the productive classes. That which is being passed on, and of which in a certain sense it can be said that it returns to the productive class, is raw material. If this movement of raw materials, however, is to have any economic sense, it must be paralleled by a movement of purchasing power. In consequence, we have a gap in the argument because it is suddenly assumed that value is being passed backwards and forwards and that in every exchange identical values are handed over, since otherwise a gain in value would have to result from the loss suffered by the partner in the transaction. If we were inclined to talk of a 'fundamental' error of the Physiocrats we should see it in this jump from raw material to value and in the view that value is merely the monetary expression for the amount of raw materials contained in commodities. This error spoiled the theory of value and exchange and barred the way to an insight into essential phenomena.

The rest of the product which alone represents a net return, neutralized by no claim for compensation, *the produit net*, falls to the landlord, who uses it partly for the maintenance and improvement of the *avances foncières*, partly for the discharge of social duties amongst which the payment of taxes is the most important. For the rest he can hand it on or, as the case may be, back to the productive and the sterile classes. The part handed over to the sterile class in its turn returns likewise to the productive class. Thus the circle is closed, all products are paid for and all yearly advances together with a part of the original outlay have been replaced.

The *produit net* has often been considered a theoretical monster which can be proved as non-existing by the most casual glance at reality. Yet this is not the case, and the argument that the net return could disappear even in agriculture is based on a misunderstanding. First of all, the existence of the *produit net* as conceived by the Physiocrats is established beyond a doubt. It is quite true that it is original production only which brings physically new factors into the world of commodities. Furthermore, there is altogether a great deal which is correct in the mistaken theory of value held by the Physiocrats. Above all they recognized correctly the tendency under free competition for prices to be pushed down to the level of costs—understood here entirely in the popular sense—they also saw just as correctly the problem resulting from this fact: how to explain the fluctuations of returns which nevertheless rose above the level referred to.[1] If they localized these fluctuations of returns in the creative force of Nature, they only saw one side of the problem, but not more so than did for instance Karl Marx; they also confused physical productivity and rise in values. In doing so they had left unexplained the most important fluctuation of value, the profit of the entrepreneur, but they laid firm foundations for a theory of 'surplus value' which, seen from the point of view of the period, was by no means so absurd. In the first place, however, they sensed correctly one tendency of the

[1] They described the cost price as the 'natural' price (Le Trosne) and valued it in a positive sense (Le Trosne called it the 'bon prix'), a point which does not concern us here. It has often been noted that the Physiocrats saw in high corn prices a symptom of wealth. The costs consist in the maintenance of the *cultivateurs* and it was this fact which explained this point of view in opposition to the popular and the classical attitude: High costs to the Physiocrats meant a high standard of life of the workers.

exchange traffic between classes and recognized the main features of this traffic clearly. Quesnay wrote with some justification: 'La marche de ce commerce entre les différents classes et ses conditions essentielles ne sont point hypothétiques. Quiconque voudra y réflêchir, verra qu'elles sont fidèlement copiées d'après la nature.' (*Oeuvres*, p. 60.)

In the theory of wages, too, they made great progress, not only in spite of their starting point but in fact because of it. First of all, the conception that all workers live on advances is in itself already a wage theory in nuce. From this basis we are bound to arrive at the arguments which were later embodied in the wage fund theory, even if the Physiocrats themselves did not achieve a precise formulation. Turgot, it is true, uses the expression *fonds des salaires*, but he talks about it only in a common place manner which lacked the characteristic content of the wage fund theory. Furthermore, from the system of the Physiocrats there emerged the 'brazen' theory of wages, which was likewise formulated in a precise form for the first time by Turgot. The Physiocrats did not merely accept a contemporary opinion already in existence, but from the foundations of their system there follows the proposition that each worker could add to the product merely the value of the means of subsistence consumed by him and that—as Quesnay himself stresses—wages settled down upon this point because of the competition amongst the workers.

Their theory of interest came off worst. In this respect the specifically physiocratic point of view was naturally most harmful, and we find accordingly that the Physiocrats showed the least understanding for this phenomenon. The gain produced by industrial capital has no foundation at all and should really have been logically described as a gain at the expense of the *produit net*. This conclusion, however, is drawn with complete clarity only by the elder Mirabeau in his plan for the abolition of industrial interests. In all genuine Physiocrats however, we find the opinion that the sole source of interest is the return from land, and furthermore that it is the fact of the *produit net* alone which makes saving—and with it industrial progress—possible. Turgot later tried to fill the gap and said many things that were correct about the establishment of rates of interests as the result of supply and demand without, however, going very deeply into the matter. In spite of his proposition that interest is the price for the temporary use of a unit of value we find that in his search for a more penetrating explanation he entrenches himself behind the expedient of all Physiocrats which assumes that competition, as it were, adds interest to capital, since the capitalist would otherwise buy land. This proposition follows from the principles of the Physiocrats, although we found it already in Hutcheson.

Commercial interest is nothing but gain at the expense of the other partner. We must make a distinction between industry and commerce in the sense in which the Physiocrats used these terms, but this distinction is never completely explained. As far as industry is concerned, there is, if not a creation of value, at least an addition of value—the value of the raw materials and of the means of subsistence of the workers having been added during the process of production—note the analogy with Marx—and its usefulness is not denied. Although it cannot be imagined why we should not be able to say exactly the same thing of trade, it must be remembered that the Physiocrats considered trade as an evil which had to be limited as much as was feasible. It is possible that in this context the popular idea played its part that intermediary trade increased the price of commodities and consequently upset, as it were, the normal exchange relation and the economic *ordre naturel*.

5. However this may be, it is certain that the system of the Physiocrats in its essential features represented an enormous advance. Even that one feature to which it owed its wholly unfortunate name did not by any means spoil everything—in this case as in so many others some disciple had considered that part of the system of the master most important which was in fact least valuable.[1] The Physiocrats were to suffer much more from the misrepresentations and quite superficial objections of contemporaries and later writers than from justifiable criticism. Most of the various objections, particularly those which were raised against their theo-

[1] It was this name which was partly responsible for the charge which to this day has often been levelled against the Physiocrats that their approach was 'naturalistic and mechanical'.

retical propositions, merely redound to the discredit of those who raised them. The inner logic of the system is to a rare degree free from mistakes and most things that at first glance appear strange and incomprehensible can be satisfactorily explained by a more penetrating study. We cannot go into this problem, however, any more than we can deal with their practical conclusions in any other way than very briefly.

The *ordre naturel* is the state of affairs which is most advantageous for mankind. Every individual accordingly acts in the interests of the whole if he pursues his personal interests. This proposition in its application to economic conditions is both valuable and false in the same sense as is the theory that the maximum of utility can be achieved by free competition on the basis of individual self-interest, which later was to play such an important role and which in substance is identical with the physiocratic position. Because of this fact and because all classes are interested in the largest possible size of the *produit net* on which indeed all progress depends, a harmonious conception of the relations of class interests with each other resulted. The favourable interpretation of the consequences of free competition, therefore, did not entirely result from the premises derived from the Law of Nature with which the argument was adorned, but from an analysis of the economic process itself. This provided the Physiocrats with a definite approach to the problems of the period, but it is outside the limits of our task to describe its high lights. We must, however, in any case name the following scientific achievements: The refutation of the belief in a favourable balance of trade, in connection with which they stressed the fact that the accumulation of money in any country merely leads to a rise in prices.[1] Furthermore, it was Quesnay already who demolished the popular catchword that tariffs were simply borne by foreign countries and who pointed out that aggressive tariffs could in certain circumstances harm the country which imposed them more than the opponents against whom they were directed. It was understandable that the Physiocrats found in these conclusions a confirmation of their fundamental belief in the ad-

[1] This merit, which represented a step towards an analysis of money, they shared with Genovesi and others.

vantages of freedom of exchange and of labour and in the harmfulness of interference by the State in private decisions concerning production and consumption. We must, however, never overlook the fact that in spite of this principle and with a correct estimate of its limits they ascribed as essential for the life process of society fairly far-reaching functions to the State (which amongst other things had to make *avances souveraines* for road construction etc.), to legislation and finally to morals and customs (particularly in the use made of the *produit net*). Conditions of the period forced them to stress the former point of view particularly strongly, but the latter was not lacking in their scientific system. Practical slogans, however, have to be brief and pregnant and cannot be formulated scrupulously. But we are not concerned here with *laisser-faire.*

Their theory of taxation contained some very important conclusions. It is based on the idea that poverty, though it is generally caused by arbitrary and violent diversions of the economic stream from its natural course, is in the first place the result of the particular systems of taxation of the period. The phenomenon of poverty, therefore, does not, as is the case in many other systems,[1] appear as an integral element of economic life, nor can it be explained by certain fundamental tendencies of human nature, but must be understood to result from acts of interference with the economic process and from external causes of disturbance. From this the conclusion followed that if the most important causes of disturbance were removed and the burden of taxation was concentrated on the *produit net* a considerable cause of poverty would disappear. This is the theoretical significance of the physiocratic theory of taxation which can claim the credit of having discovered for the first time in a systematic way essential advantages in direct taxation. Their single tax on land, however, was not allowed to exhaust the whole *produit net* because by doing so it would substantially destroy the right of property in land. In view of the importance of the *produit net* for saving (already mentioned by us), for the increase of the *avances foncières* and for progress in general this would mean that the economic system, if for the landowner the motive for cleaning and improving the soil disappeared, would be

[1] e.g. with Ortes.

harmed in a similar way as if property rights as such were limited, which would disturb the economic behaviour of individuals. In this there can be discovered the economic core of the physiocratic theory of property, while its other aspects of a sociological character and derived from the Law of Nature (the latter used in the sense of a belief in inborn rights) do not concern us here.

In the discussion of topical problems of economic policy, in which they participated and which partly caused them to develop their views, the Physiocrats and their intellectual neighbours developed their world of ideas and stepped from their studies into the fresh air of party controversy. For the Physiocrats in particular the controversy about the French corn laws, which was not merely a principal theme of economic writing, but indeed a main topic of social conversation, was the most important problem. It was in fact at this point that the two sources of economics united. Never again has the investigation of basic theoretical truths by the practical man and (shall we say) by the philosopher been separated: even if in the literature dealing with special problems both groups can, of course, always be distinguished. With this the basis for a modern theory of economics was firmly established.

6. In these discussions the voices of the scholars were listened to. Public interest turned to them and large circles sensed the need for the new science. Yet it was not easy to come to terms either with the complete and inaccessible systems of the scholars or with the multitude of investigations by people in practical life, the value of which was so uneven and could be judged only with difficulty. The period demanded a balanced synthesis of the existing elements, a reliable guidance by expert hands. This synthesis was bound to come and its product could not be arbitrary: however many people attempted it successfully and however independent these people might have been of each other, they were bound to arrive at very similar results. Yet it was difficult to solve the problem since this demanded on the one hand a philosophical-historical and general scientific training and on the other an open mind for current tendencies as well as for results outside the philosophic circle.

Two authors stand out clearly: they fulfilled these conditions to an eminent degree, they had originality and an open mind, they were able to adapt themselves and were independent and, finally, may it be said at once, they possessed that degree of superficiality which such tasks demand since otherwise the zeal of the scholar would lead them into fields of inquiry of no interest to the large public. All others who attempted the task remained stuck at some point since they merely saw one side of the problem, or they could not attract any attention at all. The first of the two authors referred to was Turgot[1], whose brilliant talent, formerly underestimated, is today so much the more recognized, indeed almost excessively so, since nothing recommends an author more to the historian of ideas than the fact that he has to fight for him. For this reason it must be said at once that if we remove the magnifying glass through which people usually look at his achievements, admittedly a great deal remains, although all the points which we could quote specifically can be found also in non-physiocratic writings, particularly in the English literature of the period. Moreover, his prestige is, at least in part, based on the fact that a great deal has been interpreted into his fluent propositions. Fundamentally he was a Physiocrat and it was on to the physiocratic system, which in spite of everything represented his daily bread, though he never really deeply penetrated into it, that he grafted other ideas which the practical life and the literature of the period inspired in him, although he never unduly worried about their inner connection. Even though he recognized in capital a factor of production, much could be said against this 'conception', apart from the fact that we find it in him in the same form as in Hutcheson and in a form which was not essentially different from that of

[1] Turgot's most important economic work is the 'Réflexions sur la formation et la distribution des richesses', written in 1766 and published in the *Ephémérides du citoyen* (November, 1769, to January, 1770). His collected works were published by Dupont (1809 to 1811) and by Daire and Dussard (1844). The literature on Turgot is very extensive. Works on the physiocratic school also deal with him. cf. further: Dupuy Eloge de Turgot, *Mem. de l'Acad. des inscriptions et belles lettres*, Vol. 45. Batbie, *Biographie de Turgot*, Mostier, *Turgot, sa vie et sa doctrine*, Ch. Henry, *Correspondence inédite de Condorcet et de Turgot*, 1882, S. Feilbogen, *Smith und Turgot*, 1892, Schelle, *Pourquoi les réflexions de Turgot ne sont elles par exactement connues?* 1886.

Locke. He had a better insight into the phenomenon of value, but he did not see it nearly as clearly as did Condillac a little later, and no more clearly than Cantillon or Galiani had done. We have already mentioned some of his individual achievements. In this context it is merely necessary to mention the comprehensive character of his efforts to arrive at a synthesis. This fact and the insight into magnificent plans which his correspondence opens to us probably justify the judgment that a life work from his pen might have become a second *Wealth of Nations*.[1]

7. The other author who must be mentioned here is Adam Smith, who achieved decisive success in a way in which few had succeeded before him.[2] He approached his task with great resources. He employed a life-time in gaining complete mastery of the philosophical-historical, to a lesser degree of the scientific and to a still lesser degree of the legal knowledge of his time. He opened the gates of his mind to all tendencies accessible to him. In him we find fewer gaps and prejudices than in any other economist with the exception of John Stuart Mill. His main works, *The Theory of Moral Sentiments* (1759), a theory of ethics, and the *Wealth of Nations*, are nothing but fragments of a range of interests, the extent of which even his remaining publications, which need not be mentioned here, merely indicate. In a letter written in 1785, he spoke of the grandiose idea of a philosophical history of all the

[1] He had, however, no influence on this work. This assumption, often expressed, has been refuted by the publication of A. Smith's lectures of the year 1763 (ed. Cannan 1896).

[2] *An Inquiry Into the Nature and Causes of the Wealth of Nations* (1st ed. 1776, a critical edition by E. Cannan, 1904). The most successful book of economic literature. The literature on A. Smith is legion. Of specialized works we may mention: of biographies starting with the one by D. Stewart the German work by Leser (1881) and the best English one (altogether the most thorough work) by John Rae. Of books on his work: the introduction by Cannan to his edition of the *Wealth of Nations* and of the Glasgow lectures, Hasbach in the already quoted work and *Untersuchungen über A. Smith* (1891), Baert, *A. Smith and His Inquiry Into the Wealth of Nations* (1858), Oncken, *A. Smith in der Kulturgeschichte* (1874), Zeyss, *A. Smith und der Eigennutz* (1889). Articles on Adam Smith in *Handwörterbuch der Staatswissenschaften* and in Palgrave's Dictionary. The *Wealth of Nations* has often been translated and many abbreviations and commentaries have been published.

different branches of literature and of a theory and history of law and government. But such great plans remained in the background and did not disturb the even course of his detailed investigations to which he devoted himself with imperturbable and genuine philosophical serenity and which he accumulated without haste while pursuing his work as a teacher. The methodical habits of the professor and scholar stood him in this respect in good stead, as did a sober somewhat jejune approach which summed up with assurance a system or a phenomenon without ever dwelling too much on details. He was not troubled by a plethora of ideas, nor was he misled by them into paths where only few would have managed to follow him. He was a man of systematic work and balanced presentation, not of great new ideas, but a man who above all carefully investigates the given data, criticizes them coolly and sensibly, and co-ordinates the judgment arrived at with others which have already been established. Thus this man with a crystal-clear mind created his magnificent life-work from existing material and by treading on familiar paths.

He expressed the spirit of his age and gave to it exactly what it needed, no less and no more. This fact and the external and internal merits of his achievements account for his success. Had he dug more deeply, he would not have been understood. His masterly presentation has been praised justifiably and yet this is not altogether a compliment. Nobody dreams of praising or blaming the style of Newton or Darwin. They stand above such merits or defects, while Smith does not. It is true that somebody once was rash enough to compare the *Wealth of Nations* with the Bible, but soon a calmer and juster estimate asserted itself. Smith suffered comparatively little from the favour or hatred of the parties; in Roscher's book we read already an appraisal to which nothing need be added. Today we can be under no illusions about Smith's intellectual dimensions since we can clearly enough distinguish between pedestal and monument. The *Wealth of Nations* resulted from a part of his lectures on moral philosophy which he delivered at the University of Glasgow during the period from 1751 to 1764 and which even in their outward form closely followed those of his teacher Hutcheson. The notes, which were produced in 1763 and have come down to us, show us that he hardly altered more in his teacher's system than any lively pupil would have done. In 1764 he went with a fairly complete system to France where he established contact with the Physiocrats. In the serene years in Kirkcaldy he added those points in their system which we have described as essential to his own so that he burst its frame with the result that symmetry suffered seriously. In this respect, however, it must not be forgotten to what extent he proved his intellectual independence and superiority in the choice of the elements which he adopted—in fact this in itself constituted an independent achievement. In the third place we must mention the influence exerted by Mandeville. Mandeville had given a grotesque form to a profound conception in his *Grumbling Hive* (1705, a new enlarged edition appeared in 1714 under the title *The Fable of the Bees*), a moralizing poem which attracted attention without being taken really seriously. In this form, however, is contained the best and most lucid presentation of the idea that the selfish interest of the individual performs a social function in the economic sphere. Now there were sufficient other sources for similar thoughts, but many a phrase in Adam Smith points to the fact that he was influenced by Mandeville in particular. Finally Smith owed much to Hume and Harris as well.[1]

We shall have to talk of Smith's doctrines in the next section of this book. In this context we merely wish to indicate the general character of his work. In his case too the critics, as was usual, emphasized above all his views on commercial policy and social philosophy. They even insinuated that his work represented a plea for free trade and 'industrialism' or that it was merely the application of speculative premises. If we read the first sentences of his lectures on the Law of Nature, we see at once that he intended to

[1] But not, as we already mentioned, to Turgot or Adam Ferguson. The *Essay on the History of Civil Society* (1767) and *The Institutes of Moral Philosophy* (1769) of this Edinburgh professor who was an intimate friend of Smith's in no way justify Hasbach's exaggerated respect for him. He was a good writer and expounded his ideas well, but he was not at all original; essentially he was a disciple of Montesquieu. Incidentally, only in the theory of the division of labour and the theory of taxation could we speak of Smith having been influenced by him, but not in decisive points even here.

establish a theory, to gain an insight into the character and function of law, so that he could at once derive practical legal norms of general applicability. It is certain that he had similar aims in the field of economics which he defines as an art.[1] Quite a different picture emerges, however, if we contemplate his theoretical efforts. There his attention is directed to the facts, and only occasionally does a turn of phrase remind us of a political ideal or a philosophic proposition, without these alien elements ever being essential.

What then was the method which he employed? It is difficult to say, since the range of his problems is so extensive. Sometimes he analyses, sometimes he merely recounts, in accordance with the requirements of his concrete purpose. He adorns his analysis, however, with individual observations and practical experiences and mixes his descriptions with theoretical arguments. For this reason it has been easy enough for each methodological 'party' to claim him as their own. He possesses a universality which was invaluable for his own concrete purpose but was bound to disappear as soon as one wanted to penetrate more deeply into one of the various groups of problems treated by him. This explains the apparent methodological contrast between him and the later classical economists which has often been emphasized. The systematic and text-book like character of his work excludes lengthy abstract investigations just as much as descriptive research into details. Smith was formed by influences of a theoretical nature and he was dominated by theoretical aims. A nucleus of theoretical theses form the backbone of his work and the greater part of the descriptive material contained therein serve for their application, discussion and exemplification. Only a smaller part form the basis for conclusions, and a still smaller proportion exists simply for its own sake because of its intrinsic interest. The first two books describe the economic process and, starting with the division of labour, deal with the problems of money, price, capital and distribution. In the third book we are offered something like an attempt at a comparison

[1] It is true that he also defines it as a science of the nature and of the causes of national wealth, as he already does in the title which obviously meant to paraphrase the term 'Political Economy'.

between the theoretical picture and the real development of facts, the fourth book contains a discussion on commercial policy, and the fifth a statement on the 'science of finance', if this German term may be applied to it. The last books also contain material on the technique of administration. All these elements are of very different value. Themes like the purposes of government and similar ones are often treated in a doubtfully speculative manner and in this particular field Smith has nothing to offer us today. Nowhere, however, is he so positive and unprejudiced as in his purely economic statements, at least as far as their most essential points are concerned. As soon as we deal with the application of these statements the over-estimation of the practical importance of his conclusions makes itself felt in a disturbing manner and it was on these applications that the critics concentrated their attack in the first place.

III

THE CLASSICAL SYSTEM AND ITS OFFSHOOTS[1]

1. We usually describe as classical economists the leading English economists of the period between the publication of the *Wealth of Nations* (1776, Smith himself is accordingly the first) and the *Principles* by John Stuart Mill in 1848. The first twenty years of this period are poor in new exploits, they are a time either of relaxation or of contemplation. Then an upward development started with vigour and strength, rising steeply to the heights of Ricardo's *Principles* in 1817. For ten to fifteen years the discussion is maintained at the level which had been reached, but then it becomes increasingly clear that the impulse has spent itself and there is only a temporary recovery as the consequence of the work of Mill. The starting point of the period is less arbitrary than is the case with most such starting points, since in fact almost all authors proceeded from the material of facts and ideas offered by the *Wealth of Nations*. The remaining literature no longer affected them vigorously, even if it did not sink entirely into oblivion, which happened to an astonishing degree. Yet it is so much the more arbitrary to establish the small elevation in the ground, which is really all that Mill's work signified in the field of economics, as the terminus. We do not intend to do so but wish to speak in this section more

[1] There is little specialized literature just for the history of this period, although, of course, the works produced in it have caused numerous discussions in practically all theoretical treatises. Compare, however, Cannan, *The History of the Theories of Production and Distribution in English Political Economy from 1776 to 1848* (2nd ed. 1903), Bonar, *Malthus and his Work* (1888), Leslie Stephen, *The English Utilitarians*, Diehl, *Sozialwissenschaftliche Erläuterungen zu Ricardo*, also *Proudhon*, Schüller, *Die Klassische Nationalökonomie und ihre Gegner*. The histories of individual problems quoted in the introductory list of books are, of course, devoted in the first place to the views of this epoch.

of a general trend than of a definite period and to follow this trend up to the present time. In fact, we propose to take not only this trend, or better the various tendencies which are comprised in it in a rather fragile unity, but also the developments in other countries, which indeed were substantially influenced by it, and finally also the scientifically most important counter currents of the epoch and unite them as much as possible into a picture from which many features will disappear, while others will stand out the more clearly on that account.

2. Doctrines not persons are the heroes of this account. The following names may be given in advance merely for guidance: The most important successor of Smith who really went further in a definite direction—for good or for evil—is David Ricardo. (Edition of his collected works by McCulloch, 1st ed. 1846, edition with notes by von Gonner.[1]) Next to him stands in many respects E. West *An Essay on the Application of Capital to Land*, 1815, ed. Hollander, 1903, and other contemporaries who thought along similar lines. It was, therefore, more the forcefulness of Ricardo's analysis and his genuinely scientific outlook than the novelty of his individual conclusions which represent his claim to immortality. He found many adherents, although the latter did not form a majority even in England. It was possible to deceive oneself as to his real position because of the tribute which the public paid to his distinguished name and because of the success for practical political purposes of arguments which had been derived from his works, while on the Continent and in America his influence was always small. The two men who considered themselves as disciples of Ricardo in the truest sense of the word—James Mill, *Elements of Political Economy*, 1st ed. 1821, 3rd ed. rewritten, 1826, and the prolific J. R. McCulloch, e.g. *Principles of Political Economy*, 2nd ed. 1830—certainly did not prove equal to the

[1] The *Wealth of Nations* was always eagerly discussed and on several occasions edited with a commentary. In this respect D. Buchanan stands out, 1814. McCulloch likewise published an edition of Smith with a commentary. Smith found a very influential commentator in the person of the leading Scottish philosopher of the turn of the century, Dugald Stewart, through his lectures and writings. (Palmerston still testified to the impression which this man had made on his numerous disciples.)

further problems that would have to be solved, although they do not deserve the disparaging criticism often meted out to them.

As they were far inferior to their master they prepared in spite of their good intentions the catastrophe which was to befall the whole school. Considerably above them rank De Quincey (Economic main work: *The Logic of Political Economy*, 1844), a man of high intellect, whose works, however, have always been caviare for the general and W. N. Senior (*Political Economy*, 1836, in the *Encyclopedia Metropolitana*), who in many ways arrived at original conclusions. Torrens (*An Essay on the Production of Wealth*), who likewise did not really belong to the 'school', although he was closer to it than he himself believed, must not be underrated either. The work of John Stuart Mill which we mentioned earlier on follows in the main the direction indicated by Ricardo, as far as its economic content is concerned.[1] Cairnes (*Leading Principles of Political Economy Newly Expounded*, 1874) is a descendant in the direct line who, as regards scientific talent, stands high above all other direct successors of Ricardo and who, starting from Ricardo and Mill, acquired his own essentially independent point of view. Mill's disciple, Sidgwick (*Principles of Political Economy*, 1st ed. 1883), and Nicholson (*Principles of Political Economy*, 1893), were subject to many new influences but must in a larger sense be considered as belonging to this group, while the leading English economist of today[2] A. Marshall (*Principles of Political Economy*, vol. 1, 1st ed. 1890) is connected with it only by a very loose tie (almost only that of filial piety) in spite of his statement to the contrary. T. R. Malthus (*Principles of Political Economy*, 1st ed. 1820, 2nd ed. 1836), in a purely economic respect, stood in opposition to Ricardo, as we shall have to discuss later. We shall also come across his theory of population to which he owes his prestige in the first place, while it is often forgotten that as an economist in the narrower sense of the word he had considerable

[1] As regards public success the *Manual* by Fawcett (1st ed. 1863), which has the same conceptual basis, for a long time equalled that of Mill. These two books formed the ideas of the overwhelming majority of the English economists in the second half of the nineteenth century until the influence of Marshall replaced them.

[2] Translator's footnote: written in 1913.

and lasting success and anticipated a great many things which were generally accepted. He who values him as a genius does him as great an injustice as he who describes him as incompetent. He must be valued as a serious worker. It is true that only Chalmers, *On Political Economy*, 1832, can be described as a direct disciple of his, who played the same part for him as did McCulloch for Ricardo. Lauderdale stands in very sharp opposition to Ricardo and his *Inquiry Into the Nature and Origin of Public Wealth* (1804) was a trial of strength which makes us regret the fact that he foundered on the same rock which has deprived so many men of ability of success: lack of training.

Two names, however, belong to the school of Ricardo, although they are usually not included in it: Karl Marx and Karl Rodbertus. We follow Marx' own wish if we include him here in this survey, which is concerned merely with the scientific and economic part of his life-work—in spite of A. Marshall's protest—since he considered himself as one who continued the work of Ricardo. We shall deal with this later. The *Kritik der politischen Oekonomie* appeared in 1859, the three volumes of the *Kapital* in 1866, 1886 and 1894 and finally the *Theorien über den Mehrwert.* The same thing cannot entirely be said about Rodbertus (*Zur Erkenntnis unserer Staatswirtschaftlichen Zustände*, 1842, *Soziale Briefe an von Kirchmann*, 1850 and 1884). Yet his basic conceptions reveal in a decisive place elements derived from Ricardo. The importance of Robertus for German economics is great, because his general attitude and many of his basic conceptions (as for instance his idea of rent) have had a great effect, even though hardly one of his concrete conclusions stood the test of time or had any considerable success with his contemporaries. Apart from this the fact alone that he struggled and worked creatively with immense sincerity and that theory in all its details was really close to his heart secured him amidst the barrenness and lethargy of the German science of the time an influence which was to last a long time and had a formative influence. From the dark background of this epoch in Germany the star of von Thünen, *Der isolierte Staat in Beziehung auf Landwirtschaft und Nationalökonomie*, 1826, shone so much the more brightly; he was indeed every inch a thinker. The introduction of the analysis with the help of the conception of the margin must be put to his credit.[1] This represented one of the most important steps in the path of economics. His basis also is the theory of the English 'classics', but he stands as an equal next to their best. Yet he hardly had any influence at all, which is already proved by the fact that even today people who in a confused manner have an inkling of his importance see his merit in all sorts of secondary matters, even in the management accounts which were contained in his work.[2]

Von Hermann, the fourth great name of this epoch in Germany, does not stand quite so much alone. His work *Staatswirtschaftliche Untersuchungen über Vermögen, Wirtschaft, Produktivität der Arbeit, Kapital, Preis, Gewinn, Einkommen und Verbrauch*, 1832, represents the culminating point of this period in the field of German economics. Little need be said about this period, not that little was being written or that it did not contain much that was good, but these books do not breathe an independent spirit and we can understand that the general public on the one hand and the most active minds on the other were repelled by this kind of science. For the rest, that is to say, as regards their intrinsically scientific arguments, these authors clearly followed the German Cameralists under the influence of the easily accessible Smith; if we leave out of account the traces left over from the Physiocrats, already mentioned by us. After having been overlooked during a short period Smith experienced a great success in Germany: Sartorius, Lüder, Kraus, Schlözer, Jacob, in order to name some of the better writers, followed entirely in his footsteps, formulating and criticizing a little differently here and there. Soden (particularly in his *Nationalökonomie*, 1805), who can claim some originality, though of a completely barren and not very attractive kind, aimed higher. More was offered by Hufeland, *Neue Grundlegung der Saatswirtschaft-*

[1] In Ricardo the marginal analysis exists only in a rudimentary form. Its importance was more clearly recognized by Rooke, *An Inquiry into the Principles of National Wealth*, 1824.

[2] Thus R. Ehrenberg managed to see in him a representative of detailed research in the field of business life. Elsewhere, too, he is often claimed as an 'Empiricist'. He *is* an empiricist, of course, as every science is empirical, but he is so in the same sense as is Ricardo.

skunst, 1807 and 1813, whose sane, even though by no means brilliant analysis of economic principles furthered the discussion decisively, and by Lotz, *Revision der Grundbegriffe*, 1811, and Storch *Cours d'économie politique*, 1815, who must be placed in roughly the same class as the French writers whom we shall have to mention presently. Rau created the text-book of the period in 1826. Hermann stands on the shoulders of those whom we have already named and towers above them all because of his perspicacity, analytical talent and originality. Next to him we may mention only perhaps Mangoldt (*Volkswirtschaftslehre*, 1868, uncompleted, in the third (posthumous) edition the appendix is missing which contains an essential part of his performance), whose books even today are worth reading. These writers were closely connected with each other and, as can clearly be seen, stood in close touch with the oldest economic theory in Germany. They formed a school which gradually, and particularly through Hermann, assumed characteristic features, especially as regards the theory of value. Ricardo had no influence on them at all.[1] He was not accessible for them and even Hermann in one passage grossly misunderstood him; for the rest the translation of Ricardo by Baumstark by its errors alone is characteristic of the state of affairs. Later, however, Ricardo's influence became more apparent, especially in the works of H. Dietzel, partly also in those of A. Wagner.

Yet this is certainly not all. Many individual achievements cannot be mentioned in this survey, any more than the specialized writings on public finance, on banking or on similar subjects. Furthermore the historical school appeared on the scene, even if its contemporary representatives, amongst them above all Roscher, as theoreticians did not rise above the level of the writers already referred to. Fichte's *Geschlossener Handelstaat* (1800) must not be considered as the work of an economic expert, since by doing so we would do gross injustice to the high but narrow ideal of its

[1] Even though this constituted a defect which speaks against this group, yet it was to turn to their advantage, inasmuch as Ricardo's analysis did not hold good in the long run—in science as in hunting it is possible to progress further by remaining behind, at least apparently.

author. The so-called romantic school—the only representative who may be mentioned in a history of our science is Adam Müller, *Elemente der Staatskunst*, 1809—and even the lively and vigorous personalities of List, von Schäffle or of Bernhardi whom we shall meet later on do not substantially alter the picture.[1]

In France matters were very much the same. A complete picture would probably be more lively, but the development of this special branch of economic science proceeded along very quiet lines, although perhaps there was a more vigorous interest in specifically economic questions than was the case in Germany. We must be brief: the impulse imparted by the Physiocrats to economic thought soon ebbed away and Smith's domination began. It is true that the man who was responsible for this 'subjection' and who has often been abused unjustifiably, J. B. Say (*Traité*, first published in 1803, *Cours complet*, 1828–9), was not a mere popularizer but a man of scientific talent who supplemented the doctrine of Smith in many respects. For this reason French economics in those days had a greater though somewhat modest degree of originality than was the case in Germany—if we disregard its lonely peaks—not to mention the method of presentation and the practical insight which bestowed on it proselytizing vigour and self-confidence. Thus it becomes understandable why Say's inheritance was well preserved amidst the storms of the time and could later bring about a transition to more modern conceptions without too great convulsions. Amongst Say's successors Rossi may be mentioned who, however, tended more in the direction of Ricardo, furthermore Dunoyer and Wolkoff, all of whom are worth reading even today. Above all the book by Cherbuliez deserves mention as it bears in many respects comparison with the work of J. S. Mill.

[1] Perhaps in addition I should have mentioned Roeslers, *Grundlehren der von A. Smith begründeten Volkswirtschaftstheorie*, 2nd ed. 1871. Moreover, two men who stood apart but were talented above the average must be mentioned here; F. J. Neumann (especially: *Die Gestaltung des Preises unter dem Einfluss des Eigennutzens*, Tübinger Zeitschrift, 1880, *Grundlagen der Volkswirtschaftslehre*, 1889), a very independent theorist, to whom we cannot do justice completely in the framework of this treatise and Dühring, *Kapital und Arbeit*, 1865, *Kursus der National- und Sozialökonomie*, a successor of List and Carey, whose talent did not make itself fully felt in our field and whose works were less recognized than they would have deserved.

The treatise by Courcelle-Seneuil, the ninth edition of which appeared in 1905, is popular even today. Less influential than the works of Say were those of Destutt de Tracy whose economic investigations, though not very penetrating, stand within a wider philosophic framework, the construction of which deserves attention in spite of the shallowness of many of its parts. This school joined up in many respects with another which must be distinguished from the former as regards its scientific basis. It is associated with the name of F. Bastiat (Main scientific work: *Harmonies économiques*, 1850), and is independent in many ways—or at least it is subject to different influences. Simonde de Sismondi also founded a school of his own. (For us his *Nouveaux principes d'économie politique*, 1819, are in the main of importance.) Although he started from Adam Smith, in essential points he went his own way. Now we could have mentioned a great many more achievements which partly within the framework of the principles of economics revealed original features, partly outside this framework arrived at new aspects of economic factors, and no account of the development of our science should pass them by. Yet it would be futile to quote further names. Altogether, therefore, there was a great deal of bustling activity in our field. Moreover, French economic science of this period, often underrated, not only replaced still incomplete views by relatively more correct ones but reached in its middle layers a sufficiently high level to secure for itself continuity of development—while German economics failed in this respect.[1]

The Italian literature did not awake until the middle of the ninteenth century from the stupor in which it had lain since the last years of the eighteenth century. Before this it had been entirely dominated by a rather shallow 'Smithianism'. The works of Gioja, Romagnesi, Valeriani and Scialoja do not have much to offer us. Hardly a ray from the great past falls upon them. Fuoco and Cattaneo offer a little more. At the beginning of the new renaissance

[1] The most important theorist of France in this period remained almost completely unnoticed, A. Cournot, *Recherches sur les principes mathématiques de la theorie des richesses*, 1838, one of the best minds that ever occupied themselves with our discipline. His chief merits lie in the field of the theory of price.

which has maintained itself until modern times we must place Francesco Ferrana (Lezioni, *prefazioni* to the edition of the *Bibliotheka dell' Economista*), who knew how to develop vigorously suggestions which he probably received from Carey and Bastiat who had a most invogorating influence. Boccardo, *trattato*, 1853, many specialized works and Messedaglia, *Della teoria della Popolazione*, 1858, and other writings, stand at his side. There followed serious workers like Nazzani (*rendita*, 1872, *profittu*, 1877, *salaria*, 1880), Lampertico and others.

In the United States people in the main followed Adam Smith after the necessary elbow room for scientific work had been won. Before this period we can look for economic general descriptions only in the utterances of politicians, amongst whom A. S. Hamilton stands out (Work, ed. Lodge, 1885–6). D. Raymond, *Political Economy*, 1820, and Th. Cooper, *Lectures*, 2nd ed, 1831, would have to be mentioned here amongst others. The thirties produced two great original achievements. The first consists of the work of John Rae, *Statement of Some New Principles . . .*, 1834, new edition by Mixter under the title of *Sociological Theory of Capital*, 1905. It had, however, almost no effect at all in spite of the quotations from J. S. Mill and of the Italian translation in the *Bibliotheka dell' economista*.[1] The second, on the other hand, which consisted of the work of H. Carey (*Principles of Political Economy*, 1837–40; later *Harmony of Interests*, 1851, *Principles of Social Science*, 1857–60, these are his most important works), had a correspondingly greater influence. Although Carey was historically as well as theoretically superficial, even amateurish, the great impetus of his general conception seemed to meet exactly what a struggling nation needed, and his intellectual fertility had a fascinating influence on his fellow-countrymen and far beyond.

In a scientific and especially in an economic respect most writings of the subsequent period were under his influence, not only those of the adherents of his political views (such as Colwell, Pechine, Smith, Greeley, Elder, R. E. Thompson) but also those of their opponents (as above all Perry, but also A. Walker and

[1] It is doubtful whether Hearn's *Plutology*, a work which was widely, perhaps undeservedly, recognized owes much to it. Mixter asserts that it does.

others). Side by side with Carey's school there appeared the school of the land reformer Henry George, *Progress and Poverty*, 1879: amongst his successors together with others Gunton: *Wealth and Progress*, 1888, was of importance. George's purely scientific achievement, essentially based on the classical writers, was not inconsiderable, and all these currents unite in the very original life-work of F. A. Walker, *The Wages Question*, 1876, and other works. His *Political Economy*, 1883, was for a long time the leading systematic work. He was an energetic and able scholar and guided American economics away from its former course.

3. As regards the outward fate of the trends sketched by us, it appears that in spite of all differences they yet had much in common. Let us regard as an example that group in which, as even our incomplete survey has shown, life pulsated most vigorously, the school of Ricardo. The eager work of the first two decades of the nineteenth century, the external impulses of which—current problems and ideas of many kinds—cannot be described here, was crowned with such success as one cannot often observe.[1] All scholars themselves were filled with pride and joy at their achievement. One part of public opinion received them like warriors who have returned victorious, another part, which disliked them heartily, did not know how to meet them with positive criticism. Their ideas penetrated far and wide, though in a distorted and misunderstood way as was to be expected. The books by Mrs Marcet, *Conversations on Political Economy*, 1816, and Miss Martineau, *Illustrations of Political Economy*, 1832–1834, prove that even in girls' boarding schools there must have been some interest in the new infallible truths. All this is understandable and there is nothing that justifies us in making jokes about it. Yet it is equally understandable that this state of intoxication was bound to be followed by disenchantment. This kind of popular economics, as it figured in the mind of the layman, was of course a caricature of scientific economics;

[1] Ricardo was placed by his contemporaries above Adam Smith. We can understand this, as he certainly penetrated farther and more deeply. Yet we shall also understand that when later doubts appeared as to the value of the direction into which his thought had led him, Smith again—and precisely because of his relative superficiality—appeared in a more favourable light. Only this must not determine our judgment of Ricardo's personality.

it did not go deep and was bound soon to make room for different conceptions, even though certain phrases survived long to the despair of more lively minds—incidentally, not without justification if we recall to mind the ideas which they had replaced.

What is more important for us is, firstly, the fact that it was exactly this popular economics which became the basis for later criticism and, secondly, that the scientific impulse soon flagged. Already in the thirties the complaint that scientific thought had become stagnant appeared in a stereotyped form in introductions to scientific works. This complaint was indeed justified. Even Ricardo's immediate successors did not correctly understand him in certain respects, much less were they able to build on his foundations. Such a state of affairs was bound to be dangerous for a young discipline: if it begins to become boring, striving talents soon turn their backs on it, without distinguishing much between the discipline itself and its representatives. The tendency to break away, already strong in itself at moments when certain foundations have been laid and are now to be extended, becomes all powerful if the leading men do not impress anybody any more and when critics have the prospect of easy success, particularly as in such situations everybody sees before his eyes the possibility of creating new foundations. For this reason classical economics even in England and much more so in Germany quickly decayed and a flood of hostility burst upon the unfortunate imitators, while the circle of the 'orthodox' became smaller and smaller. The term 'orthodox' was, and still is, employed for all those who above all clung to that programme of economic policy which was considered as having logically emanated from the classical economy. This attack was justified and understandable, yet under the influence of the theoretical interest which sooner or later sprang up there arose a particular kind of reaction which deserves mention. The attack was caused in the first place by the change in ideas concerning economic policy and later through methodological principles produced by the opponents. We shall return to this point later on. The attack, however, referred partly also to the theoretical framework of the classical system and in this respect it emanated chiefly from opponents of a different kind, that is, from representatives of new theoretical tendencies.

On the other hand, we notice today particularly in England a tendency to rehabilitate the classical economists, especially Ricardo. There is much to be said for such a rehabilitation. Not only is it necessary to enforce an estimation of Ricardo's historical achievement which is different from the usual one, but many objections to him are unjustified from the point of view of modern knowledge, or are at least they are carried too far. Yet this revaluation has its limits. The attempt to explain away all those points, which were typical of the classical doctrine and of which we disapprove today, and to interpret into it all advances of a more modern analysis is apt to distort our picture of the growth of our discipline. If some people denounced the classical economists as bunglers, some modern spokesmen show an inclination to consider all criticism as a symptom of lack of understanding. Thus it is necessary to prepare a way for a conception of their achievement which is more faithful to reality, carefully picking our way not only between the points of view that are based on political considerations, but also between tendentious scientific estimates. The best amongst the 'classics' themselves have not made this task easy for us. Ricardo's Principles are the most difficult book on economics ever written. It is difficult enough even to understand it, more difficult to interpret it and most difficult to estimate it properly.

4. It is above all necessary to bear in mind clearly that most—and all the leading—classical economists had a much narrower aim in view than some of the earlier and many of the later thinkers. Already Adam Smith did not intend to compose a social universal science out of economic material; even the *Wealth of Nations* defines its subject-matter as a specialized branch of science to be distinguished from the general framework of economic life. Ricardo set himself even narrower limits; fundamentally he merely intended to clarify the conception of what in modern German economic theory is sometimes called the economy of exchange (*Verkehrswirtschaft*) and to elucidate general forms of the economic process within this economy of exchange. There are exceptions, however, the most important of which is the case of Marx who wanted to grasp the life and the growth of the social organism as such.

On the whole we can say that in this epoch only a comparatively small and self-contained complex of problems of social science occupied all the best minds. All basic conceptions were adapted to it and the best discussions centred round it. Whatever we may think about this self-imposed limitation it is certain that we must not oppose to the views of the classical economists objections which would vitiate these views in other branches of social science. Moreover, we must not forget that this voluntary limitation led to a concentration and specialization which was a precondition for the advances that were in fact made. In consequence this limitation was at least 'historically' justified. The remaining differences as to the extent of the tasks which the various authors had set themselves explain also what many people had felt to be a difference in the methods of the individual classical economists—Hasbach in particular stressed this point forcefully. Ricardo grapples with the basic theoretical problem and appears to us for this reason particularly 'abstract'. Smith quietly seizes on masses of facts of the most varied character and in consequence appears to many as 'inductive'. In theoretical problems, however, it is possible to be less precise and profound than was Ricardo, but in essence it is impossible to proceed in a way that is different from his. In such questions Smith's individual observations are merely examples and are not essential. For the rest the differences referred to are found to be differences of presentation. Ricardo presses on in breathless haste, Smith makes his statements in a leisurely way—as it were, as a professor who knows that he must not expect too much from a reader or a listener. This difference then appears as one in principle, but we must not be deceived by this as to the underlying unity of the method employed.[1]

[1] Hasbach in particular has attacked this view and has tried to refute the alleged legend of the unity of method employed by the 'classics' by comparing their basic propositions. It is certain that the basic views of the various authors differed as did their method of presentation. Nevertheless, nobody who knows their theory will doubt that as regards theoretical problems they all go substantially the same way. Malthus has often been represented as if he stood in opposition to Ricardo as concerns the method employed by them. This is quite unjustified, since Malthus appears to us more 'inductive' than Ricardo for two reasons only: Firstly, because he worked in a descriptive way in a non-theoretical field, that of population, in which, incidentally,

In close connection with this limitation to pure economic doctrine there must be mentioned the demand for a distinction between an investigation of the facts themselves from a discussion of what they ought to be, that is for a distinction between science and politics. We meet this demand fairly universally, thus in Germany it is upheld by Jakob, Hufeland, Rau and others, in England by Malthus whose introduction to his *Principles* belongs to the best performance in the field of methodology, in France by Say and others. The best plea for a complete refusal of subjective judgments by economists, which has ever been written, can be found in Senior whom we can confront with McCulloch as the representative of the opposite point of view. Gradually under the influence of the 'classics' there developed that view about this question which seems finally to be generally accepted today and which was best formulated by Sidgwick. His statements in the introduction to his *Principles* completely agree with those which Max Weber made in the discussion at the meeting of the 'Verein für Sozialpolitik' in Vienna, except that neither the limitation of economics to a mere economic doctrine nor the basic division of analysis and politics were generally accepted. In particular, the opponents of the 'classics' like Sismondi and others could not free themselves from the old conceptions and were unable for this reason to consider the results of the 'classics' in a true light and free from the political ideas that were derived from them, while some 'classics' themselves sinned occasionally as well.[1] We may quote as an example of the nevertheless prevalent opinion Say's

[1] For instance, J. S. Mill occasionally opposed the opinion which was soon to become popular and has remained so until today, according to which economics is a machine for the production of political programmes. Compare

---

he collected his material essentially in order to verify views which he had already adopted. Secondly, because his *Principles* state historical facts as well. Yet the essence of his thought process and the manner of his argumentation is just as 'theoretical', though not as bold and precise as is the case with Ricardo. This is not contradicted by the fact that both authors (*Letters of Ricardo to Malthus*, ed. Bonar) talk of a methodological opposition. It is quite usual that scholars in a controversy reproach each other with having employed wrong methods if they have exhausted their concrete arguments. Ricardo lost patience with this ponderous opponent and the latter described anything he could not understand as 'too abstract'. That is all.

definition of *Political Economy* which we find for the first time in the sixth edition of his *Traité*, though he spoiled the simple elegance of this definition again in his *Cours complet*: 'L'exposition de la manière dont se forment, se distribuent et se consomment les richesses', or the definition given by Ricardo, who in his *Letters to Malthus*, ed. Bonar, p. 175, regards economics as an 'investigation into the laws which determine the division of the produce of industry amongst the classes which concur in its formation'. Here economics is explicitly identified with a theory of distribution which, incidentally, in itself constitutes a sufficient answer to the untenable statement, to be found already in Sismondi and in later writers, that the 'classics' had unduly stressed problems of production to the detriment of those of distribution. Senior's definition according to which economics is a science which treats of the nature, the production and the distribution of wealth, is typical in this respect. Yet we must not forget that although the conscious formulation of these views is significant and important the advance made thereby must not be overestimated. As far as subject-matter is concerned we can distinguish science from politics in the earlier writings as well. In addition we might quote J. S. Mill's definition: 'The science which traces the laws of such of the phenomena of society as arise from the combined operation of mankind for the production of wealth in so far as those phenomena are not modified by the pursuit of another object.'

It is understandable, however, that the authors of this epoch refrained just as little from 'practical applications' as did later thinkers, particularly since they considerably overrated the value of their conclusions and their significance for the concrete prob-

---

his words addressed to Lowe quoted in Jevons *Principles of Economic and other Papers*, ed. Higgs, p. XXI: 'In my Rt Hon friend's mind political economy appears to stand for a set of practical maxims. To him it is not a science, it is not an exposition, not a theory of the manner in which causes produce effects; it is a set of practical rules, and these practical rules are indefeasible . . . So far from being a set of maxims and rules to be applied without regard to times, places and circumstances, the function of political economy is to find the rules which ought to govern any circumstances with which we have to deal—circumstances which are never the same in any two cases . . . Political economy has a great many enemies, but its worst enemies are some of its friends.'

lem. It is not our task, however, to report about their attitude to the most important questions of the period. Only one point is of importance to us in this context. One view which is often expressed in Germany, even today, can be precisely formulated as implying that the theories of the classical economists were nothing else but weapons for practical purposes, that they owed their existence to the requirements of the political controversies of the period and that political tendencies were in fact the premises which determined scientific thought. Is this correct? It is certain that contemporary problems and events have suggested topics to the economist, just as it is certain that the facts which were known to the authors of this epoch have determined their thought in the same way in which every science at any given moment depends on the existing store of material; finally, it is certain that the political desires of the individual very largely determined the conclusions which he reached. Yet it is quite wrong and in addition highly unfair if we in recognizing all this overlook the objectivity of genuinely scientific work. Three criteria reveal this impartiality: firstly, we are able to prove the scientific affinity of all essential scientific dogmas, that is, we can see that and how each proposition is based on scientific arguments and can be explained by them, whether they are correct or not. Our later discussion will show this to a modest degree. It is just the inability to see this which explains the search for political and—as we shall mention presently—philosophical *arrière pensées* which we find so frequently.[1]

Secondly, the practical conclusions of the various authors do not follow at all so clearly from their theoretical premises as is often believed. In consequence, the former on the one hand can be held without the latter or vice versa, and on the other hand an essential motive for the falsification of truth was lacking. Such a falsification, however, would always, at least potentially, be implied in any subjection of the analytical process to practical purposes. In consequence we see that, although Ricardo and Marx proceeded from the same theory of ground-rent—if we disregard minor and superficial points which the two authors, however, con-

[1] This appears disturbingly also in Cannan's otherwise most meritorious work.

sidered important—they arrived at diametrically opposed judgments on landlords and corn laws. Ricardo and Marx have the same scientific foundations, while in spite of the same theoretical basis Carey was a protectionist and Bastiat a free trader. Smith's system of theses is often interpreted as a single plea for free trade and yet there were, especially in America, protectionist followers of Smith. We must close this catalogue of examples, but we must notice in addition that these practical differences can by no means be explained as the result of mistakes and inconsistencies in the authors concerned. The theses originated in fact in the neutral territory of economic analysis; the practical claims were derived on the one hand from the material of the individual circumstances of a political economy, and on the other hand from the inclinations, interests, and personal basic conceptions of the authors concerned.

Thirdly, the authors of the classical school had no uniform programme at all for which they might have taken up the cudgels.[1] This goes without saying if one takes into account all countries. Only as regards the English classical economists and their immediate disciples on the Continent does the assertion occur again and again that they were simply the representatives of the interests of the industrial middle classes. Marx himself absolved Smith and Ricardo from this charge.[2] J. S. Mill, however, was infinitely more inclined to social reforms than was Ricardo, quite apart from the period of his life when he must indeed be described as a Socialist.

[1] Socialist writers talk of 'bourgeois' economics. By this Marx (*Comp. Kapital*, Vol. I, Preface) at first meant those economists who considered the capitalist economic system as the terminus and completion of all progress and considered its continued existence as a natural necessity. Yet in this sense most economists, amongst others J. S. Mill, do not fall into this category. Already in Marx, but more so in his supporters, a different meaning replaced the one mentioned above, according to which anybody who is not a political socialist is a 'bourgeois' economist, and only now does this term imply the charge of a class attitude which was to explain all concrete results, especially all deviations from Marx' doctrine which were found in the works of the writers thus described.

[2] Later writers were not so fair. Again and again Smith is regarded as the father of 'industrialism' in the sense of a profit making capitalist economy, and Ricardo as the stockbroker who mistook the Stock Exchange for the world and to whom anything that is highly desirable is characterized by high profits. Even in economics there is hardly an example of greater injustice.

McCalluch warmly approved of the legislation of his time for the protection of labour and Cairnes was very critical of capitalist interests. It is true that the 'bourgoisie' used every thesis of the classical economists which appeared somehow suitable and quite a few that were not at all suitable. The 'classic' authors themselves belonged, as is well known, partly to the group of the 'Philosophical Radicals'—those ancestors of the modern Fabians—and were for this reason most unpopular in bourgeois circles. Of course, we must not expect them to hold opinions that belonged to a later period. In spirit, though only within the limitations of their time and country, their practical position is quite analogous to that assumed by the *Verein für Sozialpolitik.* If this was not true for all of them, it is just this diversity which proves the neutrality of their scientific basis.

5. Let us now survey the general scientific viewpoint of the authors of this period, thus describing the relations of economics with other sciences. In Germany the professorial element was preponderant (although three of the four best economists were not professors); in France it was also in a majority, while in England it was less pronounced, because even those who were entirely or at least partially teachers, like Senior, Malthus or Cairnes, display few of the characteristics of the professional teacher in their writings. Smith, as has already been mentioned, is an exception, Sidgwick is another. Amongst the German economists, though not amongst the best ones, we find some very encyclopaedic minds for whom the tradition of the Law of Nature and Moral Philosophy still determined the limits of their teaching activities, while amongst those who were simply economists there were many with a sound philosophic training, especially disciples of Kant. Yet the influence of Kant, which on the surface—as regards definitions in general, attitude towards life and State, etc.—was very noticeable, hardly influenced the concrete economic conclusions at all. We shall have to discuss the alleged Hegelianism of Karl Marx. For the rest everybody made one contribution or another to the economic work, thus e.g. Thünen contributed some mathematics. Some had some technological knowledge, relatively and surprisingly few had historical training, though speaking absolutely historical know-

ledge played its part, while almost all contributed some knowledge in the field of administrative technique and law. The attitude and the point of view of the servants of the State—often in the highest and the best sense of the term—often prevailed, but less so just amongst the greatest economists.

Amongst the French economists we cannot discover much philosophical training, but by way of compensation more inclination to and sympathy with the point of view of the merchant. Just as we discovered—not without surprise—that already in the eighteenth century in France the conception of the State and the point of view of the civil servant had had comparatively little influence, so we find the same situation in this epoch. This probably explains the greater part played by the early Socialist and other 'revolutionary' writers to whom simply a larger territory had been surrendered than elsewhere. The English classical economists present a different picture. Above all, a definite general trend of ideas, Utilitarianism, has always been associated with their doctrine. In comparison with this the influence of the 'professional philosophers' like Reid and Hamilton meant little and even that of Dugald Stewart receded into the background, though the latter was a 'side line economist' and very successful as a teacher. The roots of Utilitarianism reach far back, but it was Bentham who first turned it into a vitally influential movement. It is a branch from the tree of Natural Law, but in making this statement we must not forget that it is strictly true only with the assumption that our conception of the Law of Nature is itself accepted. Under the same assumption what has been said about the Law of Nature applies equally to Utilitarianism. The conscious will of the individual, fleeing from pain and seeking satisfaction, is the scientific nucleus of this strictly rationalist and intellectualist system of philosophy and sociology which, unsurpassed in its baldness, shallowness and its radical lack of understanding for everything that moves man and holds together society, was with a certain justification already an abomination to the contemporaries and to an even larger extent to later generations in spite of all its merits. It was from this source that many classical economists indubitably derived their sociology and the means for the satisfaction of their philosophical needs which for the most part were rather modest.

James and John Stuart Mill considered themselves as pupils and followers of Bentham, though J. S. Mill soon overcame the latter's influence as regards the most doubtful points, to a much larger extent than his amiable modesty ever allowed him to proclaim. Bentham himself wrote economic works also: *Letters on Usury*, 1787, *Manual of Political Economy*, from 1798 onwards, but already in these writings we find that his purely economic thought—the economic analysis of facts as contrasted with the cloud of dust surrounding it—is independent of his philosophy. The same is true of James Mill who was a pupil of Ricardo's as regards economics, while for the rest their relation was the other way round and it is equally true of J. S. Mill.[1] We find on the one hand that economics is that branch of knowledge in which the utilitarian conception is relatively most useful and on the other hand that its actual influence was extremely small. Thus classical economics does not form an element of a uniform philosophic system the basic ideas of which could explain it. Phrases in economic works which seem to suggest this are for the most part merely of secondary importance. Altogether it is, as is well known, an 'intellectualist' error to which the historian of ideas easily succumbs to believe that in a more extensive and intensive investigation the scholar allows himself to be guided by certain fundamental ideas which he has acquired beforehand and which he now applies consistently. Even if he wanted to, he could not do so, since his analysis leads him into unknown territory and since the dogmas based on faith pale into insignificance amongst the details of his labours. He can at best try to express his conclusions in the form of these dogmas after his work has been done. Besides, the classical economists never had such intentions. Ricardo in particular had only a very vague conception of the nature and the contents of Utilitarianism and his concrete propositions can be explained purely economically and from the needs of an economic thought process.

[1] Bentham rightly described himself as teacher and master of James Mill, but he described the latter quite unjustifiably as the spiritual father of Ricardo. He simply thought of his social philosophy, economics in his case played too small a part for him to be able to appreciate Ricardo's significance.

Two more points need to be mentioned. Firstly, the magnificent versatility of some of the classical economists. In particular it is important that they mastered many other branches of knowledge expertly and achieved success in them independently. In passing judgment on them this must be taken into account. In view of this it is impossible to sustain the charge that their vision was limited and that they did not see anything that lay outside a small complex of problems. James Mill wrote a psychology of association which I as a layman must not judge, but which exercised the greatest influence for a long time and occupies an eminent position in the history of English psychology. Many of such examples could be quoted, but can anybody compete with J. S. Mill in this respect? His system of logic, which for a long time was dominant in its field as was his economics in its own, is merely a specialized achievement which does not permit us an insight into the whole wealth of his intellectual world. Merely to be capable of understanding Bentham and Carlyle, Hamilton and Comte, Coleridge and St Simon equally well, postulates that a man has reached a level which should protect him against arrogant judgments. That he was not merely somebody who learned is proved by the most interesting conception of a 'Characterology' and an 'Ethology' amongst other things. It is possible that he cannot be counted amongst the heroes of the mind and that especially his performance in our field was not epoch-making; in fact he hardly occupied himself with economics in the decade before the publication of his *Principles*, so that this work could almost be classified as a work of his youth. Before anybody pronounces judgment on his personality, however, he might aptly ask himself whether he could possibly have achieved one-tenth of Mill's life work.

Secondly, it is especially the historical erudition of this circle which is of great importance for us, because nothing suggests itself more easily than the belief that the classical economists were hostile to historical work or at least had no understanding for it, and that it was just this deficiency which was responsible for some weak points in their economic work. First of all, however, the whole group had its special historians, amongst whom Grote stands out, so that there can be no question of an opposition on principle.

Furthermore, some of them, as e.g. James Mill, worked in the historical field themselves, *History of British India.* Finally, most of them possessed a comprehensive historical knowledge (Carlyle sent his *History of the French Revolution* to J. S. Mill for his opinion, McCulloch is said to have mastered the historical literature as few of his contemporaries did, Senior's diary reveals almost preponderantly an historical interest, etc.).

It must be admitted that the whole attitude of the classical economists towards the life of society was somewhat philistine. Although they were a splendid group of people full of enthusiasm and altruism, they lacked that kind of experience of life and that understanding for totally different ideas which are necessary not only for political judgments but also for the solution of many purely scientific problems. Hence their absolutism and doctrinairianism which often appeared almost monastic. They did not realize that many of the 'stupid Conservatives', so despised by them, or even many of the 'foxhunters'—this term seems to imply in their opinion a most damning valuation—possibly possessed in all their prejudices the elements for a picture of social reality which was more correct than was theirs.

6. The essence of their method in the economic field is to be found in the view, best formulated by Whately, *Introductory Lectures*, 3rd ed., 1847, that as regards the group of problems which were immediately before their eyes it was more important and more difficult to digest them intellectually than to collect facts over and above the amount which we accumulate in our life. Their achievements therefore were analytical and it is this which is usually meant by the most unfortunate terms 'deductive', 'abstract', 'aprioristic'. Their chief aim was to order intellectually and to clarify the day to day happenings in the economy in order to arrive at an axiomatic understanding of its basic factors. For this purpose they stressed those elements which seemed important to them, tried to imagine how things would turn out, if no other factors operated and subjected these elements to a few and simple basic assumptions which experience had suggested to them.[1] They isolated the

[1] This procedure did not appear to them at first as a special 'method'— in fact it was their opponents who turned it into that—but more exactly as the

facts accordingly and treated them in an abstract way as we would expect if we consider the aim which they had set themselves. They adhered to this method, both in fact and in expression, however, only for one complex of problems which indeed appeared of special importance to them. Wherever individual problems were concerned, as in the controversies concerning circulation or the Poor Law, they themselves seized upon all the available material of every kind. Wherever a problem emerged for which the aforementioned fund of practical experience did not appear sufficient, they did exactly what Malthus did in his theory of population. What appears as a difference of method is explained by the difference in the concrete aims of each author, though they hardly had a clear perception of the essential limitations of the analytical method. In most cases they overrated its importance and did so the more strongly the more firmly an analytical apparatus had become established which they trusted unduly.

They knew the character of this apparatus, even if at first they did not waste many words on it, with the consequence that very soon certain hostile slogans became established far and wide. They knew accordingly that this apparatus was abstract and that it was not possible to derive from it automatically an insight into individual occurrences. Ricardo in his letters to Malthus revealed that he was clearly aware of this. It cannot even be clearly stated that they considered important only that which could be grasped in general terms. Yet they did not judge correctly the extent of the gap between theory and reality, nor were they fully aware of what today is described as the difference between real objects and objects of cognition. Thus for instance they could believe that they had answered once and for all a number of practical questions. Only much later, when under the influence of disappointment methodological scruples appeared and matters were looked at more

---

only possible approach to their problem and as not essentially different from the ideas of everyday life. Thus West says: 'And other circumstances must *of course* be excluded from consideration.' If he had been asked why, he most probably would have answered: 'Because it won't work otherwise.' The phrase, 'Other things being equal', so often used, especially by J. S. Mill, likewise had the purpose of excluding non-economic factors or even all factors except those under consideration.

closely, was the extent of the 'hypothetical' character of the premises clearly recognized and were many necessary qualifications made. This was to reveal itself in the methodological works of J. S. Mill, Bagehot and Cairnes, which we shall meet later on. If, moreover, it has often been said that the 'classics' had had no understanding for the causal determination of economic facts, this statement is not quite correct either. Some of them declared, as Bagehot did later on, that they had in mind exclusively the capitalist economy or at least a modern exchange economy and thus they themselves assumed exactly the same position which was held by some historical economists (Bücher for instance); in the case of others their interest in causal determination is self-evident. Marx sharply separated out the events at various stages of development and established quite different 'laws' from them.[1] This, however, is partly too much and partly too little. In addition we have a sufficient number of statements to the contrary and it is difficult, as is the case almost always, to paint an entirely faithful picture. Yet on the whole we can say that the sound common sense of the classical economists prevented them from applying a method which was faulty in principle and that the usual objections to them are not valid.

Things are indeed somewhat different as regards the application of their method. We often have occasion to marvel at what they considered sufficient proof and how frivolously they declared themselves content with spurious explanations. Gross mistakes in argumentation linger on and even the best amongst them often slipped. This is true also of Ricardo amongst others. Even if we most loyally acknowledge his greatness we cannot help noticing that strict logic was by no means his strong point and that he did not sufficiently think out certain problems. Thus the method which

[1] John Stuart Mill correctly distinguishes between laws which are generally valid and those which are valid merely within a certain form of organization. Accordingly he already distinguishes between purely economic and historical-legal categories. Only it is wrong to ascribe the laws of production simply to the former category and the laws of distribution to the latter, since both are so closely interconnected that production is at the same time influenced by the social organization while distribution is also influenced by general needs.

was characteristic of this epoch reveals to us those features which are shown by all young disciplines during a period of initial successes: an over-valuation of the path that led to these successes and a failure to appreciate many existing obstacles which it must prove fatal to overlook. This youthful recklessness, however, has its useful side, since without it it would have been impossible to make any progress in the early stages, but it did facilitate the task of later critics who used to discharge their duties in the spirit of Torquemada.

At this time it became definitely customary to talk of economic laws. These laws, however, never implied more than statements about the inherent inevitability of certain factors of the circular flow of economic life and they were never considered to be anything else. The inevitability of these economic factors was certainly often exaggerated, but historically speaking credit must be given to these writers for having stressed it at all even though in an exaggerated form. At any rate all this does not involve a 'naturalist' approach. If some authors equated these laws with physical laws we shall be able to refute this without forgetting that such an equation does not alter their essence and does not constitute an objectively valid criticism. Let us further consider the most important meanings which the classical economists attributed to the terms 'natural' and 'normal'. The term 'natural = corresponding to the Law of Nature' occurs indeed occasionally and only in connection with 'Freedom' and similar conceptions, that is, not in an economic context. 'Natural = corresponding to the state of nature' we find more frequently, but merely as meaning: 'in the simplest conditions'. This does not imply a statement on early history, or if it does, it is irrelevant since it can be omitted without detriment to the economic argument. Often 'natural' merely means 'obvious' or 'self-evident'; if for instance it is said that capital tends naturally to be applied to the most favourable use open to it. Of greatest importance, however, is the meaning implied in such terms as 'natural price', 'natural wages', etc. Later thinkers, first of all Cairnes, usually employed the term 'normal' for this. This meant now two things: firstly, the absence of extra-economic interferences of any kind, so that the normal price is the one which establishes itself in an economy left to itself and, secondly, the actual price or wage rate, etc. which is maintained in such an economy in the long run if no changes in the basic conditions occur, in other words as if it were the aim of the factual fluctuations in the market: the centre to which they tended (as opposed to the actual market price). This does not mean that it would be impossible for some extra-economic power arbitrarily to fix prices, but only that any such interference produces certain firmly fixed and inevitable repercussions, unless something else changes simultaneously as well.[1] The term 'normal', however, had still other meanings, such as 'usual'—abnormally high wages are simply called unusually high wages—and furthermore also 'on an average'.

The constant rates of all prices and incomes are obviously the most interesting of all possible rates. The main concern of the classical system is to determine these constant rates, in other words to investigate the political economy in a state of equilibrium, an expression which at that time became more and more customary. Yet this did not mean that the 'classics' followed the natural sciences either in form or in content. Thus they intended at first to present a 'static view' of the economy to which were later added certain statements about evolutionary tendencies—a 'dynamic view'. These expressions, as well as the actual separation of the two views, were introduced into economics by John Stuart Mill who derived the former from Comte.

[1] When therefore the 'classics' for instance say that wages cannot be raised 'artificially' we must first of all add in their sense 'in the free commercial economy under conditions of completely free competition' and 'if conditions do not change simultaneously', that is for instance if quality or quantity of labour is not increased. Furthermore, the statement must be interpreted in the sense that in the event of such a rise a process starts in the economy which robs the workers as a class of their advantage. This, however, is not quite correct. All the same it is partially correct and to stress this process was historically speaking a merit, even if its importance was overrated, besides being not quite accurately described. We shall return to this later. It is true that only the historian can look at matters in this way. For large sections of the contemporaries and also for later generations the only thing that mattered was the statement that a rise in the standard of life of the working class is 'scientifically impossible'. They had asked the economists for bread and apparently received a stone; with this the break-down of economics was complete.

Already at this period there appeared certain methodological controversies which, however, we can merely mention in this context.[1] It is true that it did not mean much that theorists reproached each other with employing wrong methods and it did not alter the fact that in truth the opponents did not materially differ from each other as regards the methods they employed. Yet there also appeared some opponents of the theory who employed quite different principles. Carlyle and Coleridge fought in England—as did incidentally also the poet Wordsworth and the historian Southey, to mention only some of the more important names[2]—the 'abstract' theory on principle. So did Adam Müller and others in Germany and the followers of Saint Simon and above all A. Comte in France. While the former in doing so merely wanted to express their general dislike of the political programmes that made their appearance together with the young science of economics and must be considered as part of the general reaction against the actions and the thought of the eighteenth century, Comte was determined merely by scientific motives. He considered it impossible for economics to be a specialized discipline, since in

[1] Cf. Malthus in *Quarterly Review*, 1824. John Stuart Mill first undertook a justification on principle and a defence of this position in an article, written in 1830 and published in 1836 in the *London and Westminster Review* (included in *Essays on Some Unsettled Questions of Political Economy*, 1844).

[2] Macaulay must be mentioned here, too. Although as regards his theory of knowledge he held the prevailing views of his period, he emphatically shared the dislike of the Whigs for the Radicals and the historian's distaste for Benthamism. Although he accepted the practically most important axioms of contemporary economics he attacked (*Edinburgh Review*, 1829) the more energetically James Mills' account of Bentham's constitutional theory which indeed bordered on the ridiculous. In doing so he turned against the employment of general premises altogether. It is interesting that he speaks often enough of general principles of political science in his essays without revealing, however, what these principles were—probably they were to be found in the statements of the political programme of the Whigs in the thirties. He also speaks of social science as an 'experimental science', that is, a science the perceptions of which are essentially based on historical experiences. In later years this expression became the slogan of many who did not want to bother themselves with theory and needed a certain latitude for their convictions. R. Owen uses it in a different sense: for him the social world is as it were a world of unlimited possibilities which were to be tested by means of experiments in social policy.

his opinion each element of social life could be understood merely in its relation to all the other elements. He believed, moreover, that classical economics was essentially unscientific and 'metaphysical'. What he meant by this is evident, he simply considered economic theory as an offshoot of philosophic speculation without any basis in fact. We know that this is not correct and it can easily be ascertained that Comte had merely a very superficial knowledge of economics. Entirely like some later critics he concentrated his attention on those great basic assumptions which headed the system of economic doctrines and which certainly at first glance appear 'speculative' without considering more closely their true nature and the use to which they were in fact put. He believed that they had been derived from some philosophic system and that the remaining economic propositions had simply been deduced from them. More truth, however, is contained in his first argument, although it does not really establish a valid objection against deriving a specialized discipline from the general forms of the economic process. J. S. Mill, who for some time stood entirely under Comte's influence, quite rightly sensed what was true and what was false in Comte's position. He tried to adapt himself to what was good in Comte by clinging to an economic theory but by stressing the 'altogetherness' of social life and the need for an historical method for other problems than the purely economic ones. The method and altogether the whole social thought of Comte is basically not much less 'speculative' than that of the 'classics', indeed his speculations are not even so harmless as are theirs, because he did more than to produce abstractions, he allowed himself to be *guided* in his work by preconceived basic ideas about the development of mankind which he naïvely considered as a unit. Yet we cannot go into this theme more closely in this context. The importance of his thought in other respects was incidentally not vitiated by the fact that as a social philosopher he completely forgot his 'Postivism'. As he was later to create a different religion, which was in fact a religion in spite of everything, so he created a different social philosophy which was again in spite of everything of a speculative character. It may be remarked in passing that this social philosophy was not materially new, its roots are in fact to be found in Vico on the one hand and in Condorcet on the other.

7. Apart from the political axioms with which classical economics was associated formally and with which it seemed to be connected materially it was above all economic sociology which furnished the main target for attack beyond which the critics penetrated very rarely at all and hardly ever thoroughly. This sociology, this picture of social life which can be gleaned from the works of the 'classics', indeed invites an attack. It represented—quite unnecessarily—that pernicious relation to Utilitarianism which in the opinion of the public harmed economics more than anything else. The nations, as defined by the 'classics', were merely additions of independent individuals of unchangeable natural characteristics who were held together by economic interests. These natural characteristics the economists simply defined by the statement that each individual was guided merely by the desire for the greatest possible gain with the least possible expenditure. So much was expected from the unhindered operation of this principle that it was bound to appear in the form of an ideal. We formulate these points intentionally in the form in which they appeared to the opponents. The 'classics' themselves already formulated them substantially as assumptions, the purpose of which was to isolate certain tendencies. It is certain that by far the largest number amongst them would have realized how inadequate these propositions were for other than economic purposes if they had treated these matters *ex professo.*[1] Inasmuch as we must assume that they did not realize this inadequacy—James Mill's article on 'Government' and other subjects certainly shows that he at least was resolved to take seriously such views—we must at least take into account the fact that the propositions mentioned above could be rendered innocuous for economics by the right kind of formulation. Yet the opponents judged them as statements of facts in themselves and without any regard for the use to which the 'classics' put them.

[1] In all fairness we should also state that the 'classics' did not have a bad sociology but that in fact they had none at all. Even today many people find it difficult to realize that this did not harm their economic investigations. Suppose we believed the earth to be a disk, could we not for this reason describe one particular geographical region quite well?

The verdict in this case could not be in doubt.

We cannot describe the powerful movement which appeared at the turn of the eighteenth and nineteenth centuries or, more correctly, all those tendencies which were united by their common rejection of the rationalist interpretation of social life and which were finally to destroy the latter. This movement was only partially a 'reaction', partially it contained fresh seeds derived from entirely different plants. For us four elements of this movement are chiefly of interest: Let us call them the mystical, the national, the social, and the historical element. The significance of the three first-named elements lies essentially in fields different from our own. All four are closely connected with each other without, however, completely coinciding. They all have in common a grim contempt for the caricature of society which in their opinion the 'classics' seemed to have produced, for the craving for profits which as they believed the 'classics' preached, for the neglect of ethical considerations, and for atomism, mechanism, individualism and similar tendencies. The 'new mysticism' was a very widespread European movement, closely connected with the revival of religious feeling and with an anti-rationalist tendency in theology, to which it owed part of its external success. Its centre was in Germany. Coleridge was an interpreter of German ideas and so was Carlyle to a lesser degree. The purely scientific importance of this group was to be found in their fight against the intellectualist error. While this tendency secured some positive achievements in other fields, e.g. in those of theology and belles lettres, and thus could establish a school (Romantic School), it cannot be said that it had the effect of producing a school in the field of economics. It could give only one point of view which at the time it was strictly speaking impossible to formulate precisely—it could provide a stimulus and as it were merely raise an objection. Carlyle and Coleridge were complete laymen in economic matters and it was impossible to accuse them of failing to understand what they attacked. Similar statements can be made about the national element. It soon became a commonplace to say that a nation had a character of its own just as an individual and could not be forced into a system. We read such a statement for instance in a youthful writing by Disraeli. Everybody, except the small circle round Bentham, was bound to realize that in national questions any purely economic argument becomes almost entirely ineffective. That in every nation there exists a common fund of ideas, feelings, dispositions, etc, which is as unshakeable as are the mountains of its country, this fact puts new problems before the scholar but does not help him to solve them and has nothing to do with the problems which the 'classics' wanted to solve.

It is true that all these ideas affected economic writers as well, but as far as economic insight and power of analysis are concerned these writers could not compare themselves with the best of the classical economists. To these Justus Möser (*Patriotische Phansieen*, 1774–78, and other writings) belonged already in the eighteenth century. Yet all our admiration for the wealth of his ideas does not justify Roscher's judgment on him. (*Tübinger Zeitschrift*, 1865.)

Other writers who belonged to this group were A. Müller, *Elemente der Staatskunst*, 1809, *Versuch einer Theorie des Geldes*, 1816, and Th. v. Bernhardi, *Versuch einer Kritik der Gründe, die für grosses und kleines Grundeigentum angeführt werden*, 1849. However great the gulf is which separated the associate of Genz and Haller from the Prussian civil servant, as far as their personalities were concerned, and however different the influences were that formed them both, in a purely scientific respect they belonged together. Their criticism of the classical economists is fallacious and superficial, in the field of theory they lacked precision and a deeper understanding, although this is true of Bernhardi[1] to a lesser degree than it was of Müller, but they shared the credit for having clearly recognized the essential points of an economic sociology. What is only occasionally apparent in Burke and what we can merely guess behind his contempt for the sociological ideas of the writers of the Enlightenment, is clearly recognized by them.

[1] Bernhardi reveals at least some originality and insight by occasional remarks, e.g. that the wage level depends on the productivity of labour and that the basic error in the theory of the 'classics' consisted in their belief that only labour was productive.

In our context their 'ethical-organic' conception of economics[1] is of primary importance, the realization that the civilisation of a nation and its inner needs form a unity. Both writers also show traces of a richer and deeper psychological knowledge, even if their positive contribution to economic knowledge was limited. In A. Müller we find the idea that the 'productive forces' of a nation have an importance which transcends their merely productive part for the present, both as regards their economic future and sound social conditions. This idea occurs at this period elsewhere as well, especially in America (compare Taussig, *Tariff History of the United States*) and in France (Dupin, *Situation progressive des forces de la France*, 1827, and Chaptal, *De l'industrie francaise*), and was developed under these influences with particular energy by F. List (Main work: *Nationales System der Politischen Oekonomie*, 1840). In the latter the group of facts of national growth, so neglected by the 'classics', emerges in a most apt formulation and was for the first time applied in a concrete way which even the modern businessman, who had no use for romantic mysticism, could grasp, especially in the field of tariff policy, a fact which is well known. In this context List's contribution towards an economic sociology is of first importance, his conception of the national economy in the setting of its historical causes as the embodiment of historically unique circumstances, which he made accessible to the large public by his ingenious but reckless and extremely effective doctrine of the four stages of development. The merits of this brilliant writer and his success were very great. It is not without reason that he can claim a position in Germany which is somewhat analogous to that of Adam Smith in England, only we must not forget that it was the practical side of his doctrine which was the main reason that he was placed on this pedestal. As regards the theoretical side of his work he clearsightedly took over current ideas which in America were already common property and had been pronounced even in Germany (Nebenius, Schmitthenner, Föppl), and interpreted them brilliantly, but he

[1] In America there also was a tendency in this direction, as e.g. in the case of Raymond. Only in this case the ethical-organic point of view agreed quite well with the theory, which was obviously quite possible.

hardly created anything original. It was, moreover, his most intimate acquaintance with economic theory or at least its more popular spokesmen and with conditions in foreign economic systems that preserved him from many mistakes, misunderstandings, and narrow-minded views, but his purely economic achievements are not particularly profound. Nor is it correct to describe him as a forerunner of the historical school—except perhaps in a wider sense than would be appropriate for a history of economic doctrine—for, as regards results, there are not sufficient points of contact between him and the historical school. As regards his method he was in the first place a writer on topical questions of economic policy and in his system he was a theorist as much as was for instance Carey. It is always embarrassing to have to analyse such a splendid reputation, but it is necessary for once to break away from the custom by which scientific and practical importance are always identified and a successful pronouncement on topical ideas and scientific achievement are not differentiated.[1]

In France there were many attacks against the general conceptions of the 'classics'. Let us mention only Sismondi and St Simon. The former expresses the views of those wide circles to whom the whole spirit of the classical system was repugnant and whose dislike of the capitalist system became the motive force for a social criticism which appeared more extensive than it really was. This tendency imparts a lustre to his name that from a purely scientific point of view is inexplicable. He owes his economic training to Smith, but his historical studies led him away from the latter on to different paths. He attacked Smith's successors—and those who were under his influence did the same—principally with the ethical argument which in the way it was used by him implied hardly more than a misunderstanding of the intentions of the 'classics'. It

[1] If we had sufficient space we would have to deal more fully with one particular point in the thought of Rodbertus. He reproaches the 'classics' with having dragged into the general theory of economics historical elements which were peculiar only to individual forms of organization and with having attributed general validity to them. This charge is only partially justified, since we find already in A. Smith the beginnings of the distinction between the economic and the historical-legal categories. Rodbertus, however, was the first to formulate this distinction clearly and consciously. We find it substantially also in K. Marx and in Proudhon (*Qu'est-ce que la propriété?* 1840).

was in these circles in particular that the naïve belief established itself—formulated most precisely by Droz, *Economie politique*, 1829—that the 'classics' considered economics as an end in itself, as if the economic goods did not exist for man but man for the goods. Sismondi is particularly unconvincing as a theorist: It is quite wrong to see in his statements on surplus value more than an expression of the popular belief that the upper classes in capitalist society lived at the expense of the proletariat. Moreover, very little can be said in support of his theory of economic crises. Yet his works at least offer some elements for a conception of the economic process which is different from that of the 'classics'. Whether he can be considered as a precursor of the historical school must depend on the criterion which is accepted as typical of the latter. His relation to the historical school is similar to his relation to Marx: in both cases the historian of economic thought must be on his guard against exaggerating a relation which in fact does exist, because by doing so he will merely produce a distorted picture. Considered as a historical scholar or as an human being and as a politician in the social field this honest personality who was filled with social sympathies assumes of course quite a different place.[1]

It is often said that St Simon (Main works: *Du système industriel*, 1821, *Nouveau Christianisme*, 1825) is without any purely scientific merit, and it is certain that his importance does not lie in this field. Yet his originality and profound thought overcomes in many points his inclinations to act as a prophet. It is surprising how many of his ideas we find again later on in our science. He influenced not merely the Socialists but also J. S. Mill and M. Chevalier. For us merely his criticism of property is of importance; it is based on its conception as a changeable social institution and is far superior to Proudhon's scholastic approach in this matter. We should like to interpolate here a few remarks about this theme which has been playing such an important part in the economic

[1] In many respects Villeneuve-Bargemont ought to be mentioned here (*Economie politique chrètienne*, 1834) who was followed by a number of 'Christian' economists. His importance lies entirely in the sphere of political convictions.

literature until today, even though exact results were achieved not in the field of economics but in the adjoining field of sociology. The 'classics' simply took for granted the institution of property just as e.g. they accepted the facts of the division of labour and of free competition without discussing them much, which from the point of view of the purpose they had in mind was quite justifiable. They did not develop a sociology in the sense of a deeper insight into the social mechanism, nor did they produce a sociology in the sense of a satisfactory theory of social institutions and principles of social organization. Most of them, it is true, at the same time expressed the belief—which, incidentally, was quite irrelevant to their economic conclusions—that private property was something unchangeable, beneficial for society, and inherently natural. They did not trouble their head over much about the various forms of private property which they simply accepted in the form in which it was offered to them under the prevailing social conditions, just as they always understood by competition more or less exactly that degree of competition which in their experience corresponded to the behaviour of the respected average businessman. Only a few, like e.g. J. S. Mill, were freer in this respect. They made no statements *ex officio* about the origin of property.

In the case of the classical economists and of some of their successors ideas derived from the Law of Nature were at work and in connection with these the view prevailed that all property—including real estate property—was the result of labour or of savings. This was the view which Marx described as 'fit for a primer for children' and which we can trace back first to Locke and then further in a way which is well known. Yet this is not true of the majority of the 'classics'. As regards property of land we find—especially in Smith of whom in other respects we can say that he was more strongly influenced by the Law of Nature than were the others—the expression 'appropriation of land', which assumedly means the same thing as occupation and historically speaking would indicate a conception that was not far wrong. As regards the explanation of the remaining forms of property as the result of saving the case is worse. It is true in a sense that saving is the condition for the formation of capital—it cannot originate and increase if all products are consumed at once. Yet this goes without saying while it is much more important to ask where that which was saved first and became the foundation for further capital originally came from. From the point of view of the 'classics' the answer to this question is as follows: This original store of goods was the result of the work of the future capitalists, it was those workers and their successors who in contrast to other workers did not consume the fruit of their labour who became capitalists. This undoubtedly describes one actual process but it was merely one amongst many.

The followers of St Simon, Proudhon, Rodbertus, Marx and others opposed this theory with another which explains firstly property in land—this, indeed, does not constitute a difference from the 'classics' but is merely the positive formulation of an idea known also to the latter—and in addition it explains capital property also as the result of the position which the proprietor holds in the organization of social domination and which gives him the power to appropriate exclusively capital commodities or, as the case may be, labour for their production. This idea survived until our own days and can be found in some modern writers, but all later writers were influenced by the conception of property as a reflection of the organization of society. This was expressed most precisely in A. Wagner's 'legal theory'. As already mentioned the problem was treated historically and sociologically chiefly outside the sphere of economics (by Arnold, Letourneau, Felix and others), but these discussions nevertheless influenced the spirit of the whole of economic theory as well.

8. The 'nations' as defined by the 'classics' were not simply amorphous, they were divided into classes: The landowners, the workers and the capitalists. These classes were above all the basis for economic functions and interests, but they were no mere abstractions and were identical with the social classes as they existed in reality. This is why the 'classics' as a rule understood by 'workers' not all those whose income must be classified as wages but above all the manual workers, that is, those people of whom we think when using the term 'Labour problem', and whom we

do not simply consider as an economic category of members of the economy but rather as a social class. The conception of 'landlord' was formulated more precisely by Senior as the owner of 'natural agents'. The class of the capitalists is essentially characterized by the fact that they employ workers, provide the materials for work and advance the means by which the worker can be maintained.

At first it was only Say who distinguished in addition a special function of enterprise. Great credit is due to him for this, but later others followed him, amongst the English J. S. Mill first of all. Yet to this day people have continued to confound the two functions of capitalist and entrepreneur. None of these writers attempted a more detailed analysis of the phenomenon of class, in particular of the causes of the origin of classes, nor did they try to investigate those partially extra-economic elements which make classes into units that proceed together, though it is in these elements that the deeper significance of the formation of classes is to be found. Only Marx made such an attempt and it is from the circle of his followers that the assertion emanated according to which the economic element represented the essence of the phenomenon of classes—the other writers did not commit themselves in this respect.

The exact investigation of the phenomenon of class belongs to a later period and was promoted in the first place by sociologists but also by economists (Schmoller, Bücher). Carey and Bastiat tried to prove that there existed a harmony of interests between the economic classes, while in the case of Smith and Ricardo the opposite point of view is stressed. Yet this does not constitute a particularly strong contrast but is rather a difference in emphasizing the individual groups of facts: the relations between the classes are so manifold that common and opposing interests are almost always present simultaneously, and whether the one or the other is stressed depends on the attitude which has been adopted by the observer. The idea of the class struggle as a principle explaining social events was first stressed with full vigour by Marx while we find approximations to it only in the early Socialist literature.

The general picture of the economic process, sketched by the classical economists, does not lack an historical element. Yet in accordance with their analytical purpose this element is merely mentioned in passing (cf. for instance J. S. Mill, ed. Ashley, p. 20). Their economic picture can usually be divided into a theory of production, of circulation, and of distribution, to which as often as not—sometimes in the place of the theory of circulation—must be added a theory of consumption. The rudiments of this system can be found already in A. Smith, it emerges clearly in Say and about the same time also in Germany. This system remained decisive for the subsequent period, only later a chapter on the 'conditions' of the economy was added when the interest in the sociological foundations increased. A system that was definite in all its details did not develop, however, and these remarks are valid only approximately. In Germany very soon a distinction emerged between economic doctrine and economic policy, or between general and applied economics, and this distinction remained the rule in Germany while it met with little approval outside it. The doctrine of the three factors of production can be ascribed also to Say and is not simply contained in Smith already. It very soon became prevalent in Germany but gained ground only very slowly in England. It assumes an original form in the writings of Senior who describes labour, natural agents and abstinence as the three factors of production. Most of the 'classics', however, show an inclination either, as Petty had done, to accept only two original factors of production,[1] or merely to treat labour as such a factor—therefore, they identified 'producers' and 'workers'.

The importance of these views differs from author to author and can often be judged only with difficulty but we cannot go into this more deeply. Most of the writers of this period cling to the physiocratic conception of 'advance'—only that the advances which the workers receive and which furnish the means of production emanate merely from the capitalists and not also from the landlords as was the case with the Physiocrats—and there arose very little opposition—especially in Germany—against this conception. They also clung to the conception of the social product and its distribution. As regards details of the conceptions of the

[1] J. S. Mill did so for instance. Today this view is becoming generally accepted under the influence of Böhm-Bawerk.

social product, social income, and social capital we must refer here to the relevant histories of economic doctrines. Only one point may be mentioned. Rodbertus (*Das Kapital*, pp. 78, 230, and others, e.g. Held, *Die Einkommensteuer*, 1872) charged the classical economists with having neglected the social conception of income and capital and with having occupied themselves too much with individual income and capital instead of treating them as social units. This is not quite correct and is not true at all of Ricardo. It was John Stuart Mill who first introduced into English economics the 'point of view of the entrepreneur' which had been first upheld by the French. Even this, however, was not done in order to honour the entrepreneur or because his welfare was considered especially important but simply because the entrepreneur stands at a place in the economy from which it is possible to have a wide view over its processes and because his deliberations form a very important motive force in the economic nexus. Incidentally, there is no contradiction in principle between the two approaches.

The guiding principle of classical economic theory was that of self-interest. It was only a minority of authors who formulated it expressly—they did this in fact in different forms—thus for instance Senior and John Stuart Mill. Originally we met it in Adam Smith as the fundamental motive of economic man. Smith teaches that we expect our bread not from the benevolence of the baker but from his self-interest (cf. for this also Reinhold, *Die bewegenden Kräfte der Volkswirtschaft*). Later on the principle changes its character and becomes an assumption designed to characterize a certain type of action or its content by becoming the 'economic principle' *par exellence*. Already in its original form popular objections to it did not deprive it of its basic importance. In its later form it no longer contained even the shadow of concrete statements. The economic principle, however, is not fit to form *the* characteristic element of an economic system, as no discussion of economic matters can do without it. We may limit it, we may formulate it very differently and if necessary cut it out altogether from our description, but consciously or unconsciously we must always make use of it—even in an historical account of economic matters. Two other propositions, however, are not only of great but also of characteristic importance for the classical conception of the economy, the law of the diminishing return from land and the 'principle of population'. Neither of these two propositions is purely economic and in this sense indispensable for an economic theory: the former formulates a technical fact, the latter a point of the human part of the history of nature.

Although we find the law of diminishing returns from land already in the eighteenth century in the scientific literature of the time (Turgot, Ortes), in the English discussions on economic policy of the early part of the nineteenth century (*cf. Cannan, loc. cit.*) we meet with the opposite view that increased capital expenditure in agriculture as well as in industry is accompanied by a fall in cost per unit. It was only through the efforts of Anderson, Malthus, West and Ricardo that the view prevailed according to which there existed in this respect an essential difference between agriculture and industry and that for the former the law of diminishing returns is valid, while for the latter the law of increasing returns operates. We shall touch on this theme when we deal with the theory of ground-rent and should like to state here merely that the proposition of diminishing returns or rising costs per unit in agriculture played a considerably smaller part in the French and German literature than it did in England. It was attacked in principle only on rare occasions and without any success—these attacks, it is true, have continued into the present—yet it was more its value for economics than its objective truth that was called in question.

Now with the classical economists the proposition had two completely different meanings. First it was intended that it should express a general fact which could be observed in the daily operation of any economic system. Any further expenditure of equal quantities of capital or labour on the land would yield a smaller return, gross or net, provided the method of production remains the same. This limitation is necessary: any improvement of methods annuls this tendency during the period of transition to them. In this respect there exists in the classical economists and especially in Ricardo a definite parallel between expenditure on capital and on labour. If the number of workers is doubled it is necessary to double capital expenditure as well. If we drop this parallel connection we are unable to accept certain of Ricardo's conclusions. The 'classics', furthermore, did not waste any thought as regards the scale of the diminution of returns in various countries, on various estates and with various kinds of cultivation on the same soil, but simply assumed it to be the same in all these cases. Out of this certain objections develop which, however, do not affect the essence of the matter and which can at best enforce an improvement in the formulation of the proposition. Moreover, the leading 'classics' were of the opinion that finally the limited supply of better types of land and the increasing difficulties of producing more on all types of land would make further improvements in production impossible and in consequence any further extension of production of food would meet with insurmountable obstacles. While the law of the diminishing return from land in its first sense was an important tool of theoretical argumentation, in this second sense this was no longer the case as it merely had become a more or less interesting prognosis of what would happen *concretely* in future. All the more important, however, was this second meaning for the total character of the classical picture. It alone bestows on it that 'pessimistic' trait which has been stressed so often—and in so many cases unjustifiably—and which explains the attitude of the 'classics' to many practical questions. It also explains why they stressed certain facts and developments while they neglected others.

Economists have been interested in population problems from time immemorial and it was always the two points of view of the importance of a large increase of the population for national greatness and the development of civilization and of the danger of 'overpopulation'—defined very differently—that came to the fore. The former point of view prevailed until the middle of the eighteenth century, but even then the latter was not absent. Already Botero, *della cause della grandezza della citta*, 1589,[1] said that the *virtus nutritiva* decreased progressively while the *virtus generativa* re-

[1] Botero influenced Adam Anderson (to be distinguished from James Anderson whom we have already mentioned and shall have to mention again), *An Historical and Chronological Deduction of the Origin of Commerce*, 1787–89 (completed by Courbe).

mained the same. This view becomes dominating with the Physiocrats. Quesnay, who converted Mirabeau to it, who originally had considered an increase in the population as the decisive motive force in the growth of wealth, wrote: 'La population n'a de borne que celle de la subsistence et ella tende toujours à passer au delà', a phrase which already contains all that matters. Beginnings in this direction we find already in Genovesi, Turgot, Stewart and others, while in Ortes we already find the formulation which has become so famous, according to which the population tends to increase in a 'geometrical ratio' while food tends to increase merely in an 'arithmetical ratio'. Moreover, Townsend, *A Dissertation on the Poor Laws*, contained in Overstone's, *Select Tracts*, 1859, argued in exactly the same way as people were to argue later against the weakening of the brakes on an increase in the population. In his opinion such brakes were involved in Poor Law legislation and were provided by hunger as a penalty for reckless propagation.

All this does not detract from the subjective originality of Malthus, since he hardly knew any of these precursors, although he did know one of them, namely Wallace, *Various Prospects of Mankind, Nature and Providence*, 1761, who, however, had not gone into the matter quite so deeply.[1] When in 1793 Godwin published his *Enquiry Concerning Political Justice and its Influence on General Virtue and Happiness* Malthus opposed him, *An Essay on the Principles of Population*, 1798. Godwin in the spirit of Condorcet had told fairy stories of the unlimited possibility of perfecting human civilization and of forming the mind of man which in itself was quite colourless and could be shaped quite unhampered by circumstances since it was in principle identical in all individuals. Neither Godwin[2] nor Condorcet nor their successors, to

[1] A controversy about the size of populations in the ancient world had developed between Wallace and Hume in which the question of the increase of populations had been treated in many passages and which influenced the problem considerably.

[2] The 'agrarian Socialist' Thomas Spence, *The Meridian Sun of Liberty*, 1776, could also be mentioned here as one of the many representatives of the egalitarian systems of the period. We cannot deal more closely with this literature the scientific importance of which is very small. Compare P. Gutzeit, *Die Bodenreform*, A. Menger, *Recht auf den vollen Arbeitsertrag*, Held,

whom amongst others R. Owen belongs, are of interest to us here, but their literary success was very great. Nobody—not even Malthus—was at that time in a position to grasp clearly the basic errors of this conception which are contained in their entire psychology and sociology. People were rather forced to agree with this conception since its foundations were in keeping with the whole contemporary trend, but soon enough they stumbled upon the external obstacles which stood in the path of this progress which in principle was supposed to be unlimited. Malthus stressed one of these obstacles clearly: the increase of the population while there was only limited room for an increase of food. In doing so he at first overshot the mark: he spoke of vice and misery as the only possible restraints. In the second edition which appeared under a slightly altered title the term of 'moral restraint' was added (1803). Now the theory assumes the form that the population tends to increase beyond the food producing capacity, and misery and vice are bound to become its lot if 'moral restraint' did not operate. Malthus places no importance on the mathematical formulation which accords with the one employed by Ortes since this formulation merely represents a rough summary and generalization of contemporary conditions. It is impossible for Malthus' achievement to appear to us in the same light as it did to some of his contemporaries. All he did was to formulate precisely an idea which already existed and which was, as far as it was true, rather commonplace. Darwin's statement that he derived a stimulus from Malthus' work can hardly add lustre to the latter in view of the fact that none of Darwin's decisive ideas were even hinted at by Malthus while all such ideas go back to different sources (E. Darwin, Buffon etc.).

In estimating the importance of the principle of population for economics we have to make the following distinctions: for the theoretical essence of the classical system it is of no importance at all since this system would remain what it is, even if the principle of population were omitted from it. It is, however, all the

---

Zwei Bücher zur sozialen Geschichte Englands, 1881, G. Alder, introductions to the editions of the *Hauptwerke des Sozialismus u nd der Sozialpolitik*, Niehuus, *Geschichte der englischen Bodenreformtheorien*.

more important for the exactness and the apparently practical value of some conclusions. In those cases where pure economics by itself can only produce some general determining cause and can say nothing about concrete developments, as e.g. with regard to wage rates, there occasionally the population principle comes to the rescue and leads to statements of the desired precision and of a sufficiently concrete character. Naturally, however, it can do so only if the limitation applied by Malthus himself is taken as lightly as possible; for moral restraint, if effective, hinders the pressure of population against the existing means of subsistence and thus destroys again any chance of making definite and concrete statements. Such statements were in fact made by some economists, above all by John Stuart Mill and McCulloch, and it was their fault when later critics produced objections which Malthus himself had taken into account already. Such critics made themselves heard very soon. Thus Godwin gave his reply in 1820 in his book on population. The limitation of space for food production was denied or pushed forward into a distant future (Hazlitt, *A Reply to the Essay on Population*, 1807, many others have followed since), or it was strictly denied that a population has the tendency to increase beyond its food producing capacity.[1] Or it was pointed out that an increase in the population in itself contained some compensating factors such as a higher capacity for production, the possibility of a better division of labour, etc. Everett, *New Ideas on Population*, 1823; this argument has often been used since. As an objection this line of thought was quite unjustified. The 'classics' and their successors stuck to Malthus but they did not go substantially beyond him. Amongst the opponents, too, with whom we cannot deal in detail, the same ideas were later repeated again and again. After a period of hostility a feeling which was more friendly towards Malthus developed towards the end of the nineteenth century, but at the same time also an increasing indifference to his

[1] Gray, *Happiness of States*, 1815, Sadler, *The Law of Populations*, 1830, puts forward the proposition that the increase of the population stands in an inverse ratio to the existing number—a very bad formulation of an idea which is not altogether unsound and which in its way is not much more fallacious than was Malthus' idea—yet this book, which was very unreasonably reviewed by Macaulay amongst others, had no success.

problem within the framework of economics.[1]

9. The internal structure of the theory of this period cannot be described briefly with the thoroughness which alone would lead to a complete understanding of it and our picture must remain incomplete and only half true. Above all we must remember that almost all theorists of this epoch proceed from the first two books of Adam Smith whose system remained decisive for the subsequent period. Attempts were also made to unify and to analyse more deeply the store of facts and ideas which is contained in these books. Certain things, for instance the treatment of the division of labour—which was slightly improved upon only by Mill and was looked at from a different point of view only by some thinkers, especially by 'nationalist' writers, and was really reshaped only by the representatives of the historical school (Bücher)—remained almost completely unchanged. Other important points, such as e.g. the concentration on the annual social product of the economy and the idea of the 'distribution' of this social product, which Smith had learned from the Physiocrats, have been retained to this day. Nevertheless, within a very durable framework much was changed, in particular the theory of distribution. Smith had recognized correctly how fundamentally important it was to single out from amongst all 'market' prices that one 'natural' price which constitutes the centre of all the fluctuations of the former. When asked which were the circumstances to which the natural prices owed its relatively constant character he answered that the latter was just sufficient to secure to all those who shared in the production exactly the ground-rent, the wages and the profit which induced them to repeat the production to the same extent. The natural price, therefore, can by definition be broken up into those three elements which together form the costs of production and the amount of which determine its level. Thus the idea automatically offered itself that the entire social product could be broken up into these three elements just in the same way as is the case with individual prices. The collection of remarks on the causes

[1] Compare also: J. Garnier, *Du principe de Population*, 4th ed. 1837, John, *Die jüngste Entwicklung der Bevölkerungstheorie*, 1887, Messedaglia, *La Teoria della popolazione* . . . 1858, Quetelet, *Physique Social*, 1835.

that determine the elements of price to be found in Smith's various chapters on wages, rent and profit, at the same time represented a complete price theory as well as a theory of distribution. This was not simply 'wrong' but so superficial that people were not satisfied with it but attempted to clarify the matter in principle by seizing on one or the other hint thrown out by Smith and by holding on to it consistently. In all this discussion the problem of distribution stood in the foreground of interest.

Two tendencies can be distinguished. One took seriously the close connection between price of production and size of income and elaborated the parallel between elements of price and branches of income in such a way that the explanation of each of the latter resulted from the productive role played by each of the three factors of production, that is from the 'service producteur' of each of them. This group, led by Say, comprised most French authors and, led by Jacob, Hufeland and others, included most German authors, in particular Hermann. In England it comprised above all Lauderdale, in a certain sense also Malthus and later Maccleod.[1] In generalizing an expression which first had become customary for the theory of interest we can describe this *modus procedendi* as the productivity theory of distribution. This theory was accepted, at least basically, also by Bastiat and Carey, though they formulated it to some extent in their own peculiar way. It was later accepted by Ferrara and by many Americans, especially by Perry who followed the thinkers mentioned above. Taking into account the present status of our discipline and in view of the inherent consistency of this theory we should really accord first place to it. Since, however, the lamentable incompetence of some of its representatives led to numerous mistakes and, worse still, to many trivialities, and since on its basis no short, precise and practical conclusions could be established—not in spite of, but because of its correct procedure—this theory was for a long time—at least up to John Stuart Mill who represents a pivotal point—overshadowed by the other theory the most important representatives of which are Ricardo and Marx. This happened, although anybody who is

[1] *Elements of Political Economy*, 1858, in addition other works, especially on credit and banking.

unbiased cannot fail to sense the convincing simplicity of its basic idea.

It is essential, particularly if we want to understand Ricardo—and inasmuch as he represented the pillar of this group, this whole trend altogether—that we clearly grasp that for him there was one question which was of greater interest than any other, namely, which concrete and purely economic factors determine the relative size of the various branches of income. Strictly speaking he does not have a theory of value or of price in our sense of these terms and he developed a theory of money only as a side line; moreover, he does not really have a theory of interests or wages or rent either, in the sense that he intended to investigate the essential features of these phenomena. He intended to present a theory of the general and economic causes that determine wages, rent and 'profit', he wished to indicate under which circumstances and how they change and with what objective facts of the economy—movement of population, price of corn, composition and quantity of capital, etc.—they could be connected. In doing so he did not consider it necessary to explain exactly those branches of income or to investigate in great detail the mechanism with the help of which that definite state of affairs is accomplished which in its objective manifestations was before his eyes. What he required for his purpose he took from certain empirical propositions which were quite unconnected with each other, such as the one concerning a general rate of profit, so that his doctrinal system, though based on a fundamental tendency, yet forms no real unity. He jumped over basic problems in a way similar to what happened to other sciences in their early stages, and where these problems nevertheless came his way he took as it were recourse to local resources.

Thus he was often content with approximations with which occasionally he was not satisfied himself. In a way he strangled the vital connection between the value of the product and that of the means of production with his concrete causes which determine the various branches of income. He believed he could do this so much the more easily since it was never the absolute value of the product and of the means of production but always the relative amount of the various forms of income in relation to each other that formed his basic problem. These statements explain many of his conclusions and views. Yet if from this a defence against many attacks on him results, there are other objections that spring from the same source. Thus we might mention straight away that in spite of what has just been said Ricardo occasionally cannot help talking about the absolute size of the quantities with which he is concerned. In this connection he himself does not always notice that he had shifted his ground and his critics noticed it even less. It is this tendency which we want to describe above all in the following pages.

10. Adam Smith had placed the determination of prices in the centre of theoretical speculation and this position remained secure in subsequent years. Ricardo likewise was looking above all for a criterion for the exchange relation and its changes. He probably felt that the argument of the sixth chapter of the *Wealth of Nations* would inevitably lead to a vicious circle if it were applied consistently. Yet at the same time he approved of the first sentence of this chapter that in primitive conditions, that is, in conditions in which no accumulated capital or land property exists, it is the quantity of labour contained in the various commodities which must determine the exchange relation and he now investigates on his own how matters stand if accumulated capital and land property do in fact exist. First of all he moved two difficulties out of his way, that of the difference in quality of labour by pointing out that the different kinds of labour soon crystallize into a firm relation of values, so that they can all be as it were reduced to one type of 'normal labour'. Similarly he dealt with the fact of the uneconomical use of labour which does not determine its exchange value, by stressing the 'necessary' or 'customary' quantity of labour (Marx' socially necessary labour). As regards these two points he followed Smith. He also dealt with another difficulty which results from the existence of a second original factor of production by his refusal to recognize that this second factor renders a productive service and by taking into account basically those quantities of products for the production of which no rent is paid. In other words, he took into account only land that carries no rent and such land in his opinion is always available. By doing this Ricardo

achieves that his basic law of exchange which equates the exchange ratio of two commodities to the relation of the quantity of labour contained therein is not affected by the simultaneous operation of another factor of production. Moreover, he manages to simplify considerably the problem of distribution, since there is now only one quantity of production for which not three but only two types of claimants need be considered.

The use of fixed capital, however, effects a deviation in the determination of value for two reasons. Firstly, a change of wages will obviously affect in a different manner the prices of those commodities in the production of which capital of differing composition as regards constant and variable capital is employed.[1] This change will affect equally only the prices of those commodities in the production of which capital of the same 'organic composition' (Marx) has been employed. The only prices that are not affected at all by such fluctuations are the prices of those commodities the producing capital of which has the same organic composition as the producing capital of the commodity which serves as money.

Secondly, the employment of fixed capital carries with it a prolongation of the process of production and in consequence, as experience teaches us, the necessity for the payment of interest for a longer period and, since this period is different in the various branches of production, a further deviation from the original law of exchange. What then is the importance of this law for an understanding of the capitalist economy if Ricardo himself realizes quite clearly that it is not valid? He himself answers this question: the original law of exchange is valid nevertheless approximately in the capitalist economy. According to him wage fluctuations have only an insignificant effect on the exchange ratio of commodities in comparison with their primary cause of determination—the change of the quantity of labour necessary for production. Furthermore, a commodity the production of which requires twice as much time

[1] These are Marxian expressions, Ricardo's terms 'fixed and circulating capital' are not quite the same thing, yet this is of little importance for those matters which can be discussed here at all. Besides, Ricardo would have acknowledged Marx' distinction as more correct even from his own point of view. Marx quite rightly places great importance on this distinction. (Variable capital is wage capital.)

as another, if the necessary quantity of labour is the same, must have a higher exchange rate than the latter—but nevertheless it could on the whole be assumed as probable that two quantities of commodities which cost the same would also contain the same quantity of labour. Although Ricardo fully recognizes that the exchange value of a commodity depends both on the time required for production and on the quantity of labour,[1] the latter factor in his opinion is by far the more important and is almost decisive by itself, if changes in the exchange value have to be explained. Thus the 'original law of exchange' embodies in spite of everything a great average fact, in comparison with which all facts that are not covered by it represent deviations from the rule. To this extent the quantity of labour embodied in the commodities, its 'real value', is in fact an index of its exchange value and at the same time its 'regulator'. Of course, the monetary value of the quantity of labour is by no means equal to this exchange value.

The quantity of labour, however, is not the cause of the exchange value. This Ricardo never maintained and Mill's youthful essay (Review of Bailey's book, 'Critical Dissertation on the Nature, Measure and Causes of Value', *Westminster Review*, 1826) expressed this point clearly. On these foundations a great many of Ricardo's conclusions are based. In estimating them we must bear clearly in mind the large number of assumptions that must be made in order to render acceptable this picture of the economic process which, as his creator himself believed, explained entirely only one amongst many possible cases, even if this happened to be the most important one. In this context three things must be considered. Firstly, whether Ricardo's scheme is unexceptionable in itself on his own assumptions. Secondly, whether his assertion is correct that the deviations from his scheme are in fact of comparatively small importance. Thirdly, whether it is sensible to keep to his original law of exchange, even if reality hopelessly deviates from it, perhaps because the circumstances which are the cause for things being different do not in reality alter the fundamental principle of

[1] Ricardo does not deny the existence of other causes determining prices. Only he believes that their effect in most cases is the same on all prices and accordingly they do not affect 'relative values' very much.

capitalist economy. In fact, it could not be regarded as disastrous in itself if Ricardo's conclusions were valid only on the assumption of an equal organic composition of capital and of equally long periods of production in all branches of production because such an economy would still be a capitalist economy with all its typical characteristics. Or perhaps it might be argued that the circumstances referred to above and their effects could be grasped and judged only with the original law of exchange as a background. However, we cannot discuss this point in greater detail.

The same points can be made with regard to the construction offered by Marx which in its principles is the same as Ricardo's.[1]

[1] It is not possible to produce a penetrating analysis of Marx' life-work within the framework of this study. We cannot talk here of those points on which his importance chiefly rests, of the enormous vigour with which he created an arsenal of ideas for a political party and a host of slogans which could be used immediately and which were of magnificent effectiveness, of the glowing passion which fascinated members of his party and his opponents and of the tone of the prophet which made his work unique. This above all accounts for his success and lifted the discussion of his system out of the realm of science proper. We see in Germany a number of well-drilled writers with the zeal of religious orthodoxy in his service. To the disciple the opponent appears *ipso facto* as a criminal whose wickedness is surpassed only by his hardly credible stupidity. After every single controversy the faithful issue a bulletin of victory, every counter argument is accepted with derisive laughter. Yet it would be unjust to deduce from this on principle the unscientific character of Marx' work or to assume that his thought can be derived simply from his political aims. It is true that the agitator shouts and gesticulates on every page of his work, but underneath this form there is sound scientific work; it is true that many practical conclusions are arrived at somewhat violently, but this does not effect the core of his doctrines; finally, his polemics are undoubtedly grossly unfair, but in most cases accusations and aspersions envelop a definite argument of a purely scientific nature.

In this context, therefore, his work is of importance only as far as it is conscientiously based on comprehensive knowledge. Many economic writers with their predeliction for philosophic relations and influences have occupied themselves largely with Marx' relation to Hegel and have probably for this reason considered Marx' method as something special. If Marx in fact had borrowed elements of thought or even merely his method from metaphysical speculations he would be a poor devil, not worth taking seriously, but in fact he did not do so. He himself explains the matter in the introduction to the second edition of the first volume: in his study he was concerned not with metaphysical premises but merely with observing and analysing the facts—true or false ones. Only he had acquired a liking for Hegel's terminology which indeed is infectious and in the manner of his presentation he gave free vent to this inclination. For his success this fact was not without importance. Without the philosophic garb and the obscurity of some phrases, which is so beloved by the congregation, he would not have been so effective and inspiring. Yet for the essence of his argumentation this garb is irrelevant and it would be easy to adorn his ideas with quite different philosophic ornaments.

That Marx did not deceive himself and that this statement is correct we can see from the fact that all his positive conclusions derive from other, that is, economic sources. The Hegelian may be pleased with Marx' 'dialectical method' which explains the development of facts by the development of conceptions, the Anti-Hegelian may see in it a defect, it does not affect the heart of the matter. On the other hand, Marx' method was not an historical one either, as Engels maintains, for the only element that could support this statement, the distinction of various stages of development in which—though only partially—different 'laws' are valid, Marx shares with the 'classics', though the latter attached a greater importance to it. Nor does Marx possess a special 'objective method', for such a method does not exist at all—fundamentally it is merely a phrase, since there are objective elements in every economic argument as well as subjective ones—even in Marx. As far as possible every economist uses the former, unfortunately, however, he cannot always manage with them.

In the work of the *scholar* Marx we have to distinguish between a sociological and an economic part—however disagreeable such a distinction may be to his disciples. The economic conception of history is the *pièce de resistance* of Marx' sociology, that great idea which appeared to many as the most successful step towards a scientific comprehension of historical events and still is considered as such today. Marx' credit has probably little to fear from the claims of priority put forward by others but more from the fact that what was new in his theory was merely the precision with which he formulated the connection between conditions of production and social organization. Yet it was just this precise formulation—in particular the emphasis given to the causes of the conditions of production—which did not prove tenable in the long run. If, however, the economic conception of history must take its place amongst other elements, a general theory of history becomes impossible, and it is detailed research which claims our attention again. This does not detract from the greatness of the attempt and from its importance as a milestone on the path of science.

For us Marx is only of importance as an economist. If we try to ascertain the basis of his thought we are conscious of the fact that his subjective originality is as great as anyone's. His predecessors mean as much as they meant to him only to a person who is of the same calibre and has the elements of their achievements already within himself. We can deny Marx' originality only in the sense in which we can deny it to anybody, and he did not only possess originality but also scientific ability of the highest order. An idea like the one that modern income from interest is in essence similar to the rent of the feudal landlord—whether right or wrong—marks its author as a man of scientific talent even if he never had had another idea. Theoretical analysis was second nature to him and he never tired of working out its details. This fact also contributes to his success in Germany. At the time when his first volume appeared there was nobody in Germany who could have measured himself against him either in vigour of thought or in theoretical knowledge. Even today every teacher of economics can see from the superiority of those students who have used him as their model to those who have no theoretical interests what an educative effect familiarity with a theoretical system has—regardless of its good or bad points. Thus Marx was bound to become a teacher even of many who were not Socialists, although it is true that he did not always meet with a deeper understanding as far as precisely the scientific core of his work is concerned.

This scientific core is derived—on this the main stress has been laid above—from Ricardo. The family relation would become even more obvious if Marx had not often unduly stressed deviations of a secondary nature and had not adopted at several points formulations which deviated more in appearance than in reality. The system of the Physiocrats had a strong influence on him, more in a general way than in definite points. Yet one tendency in English literature which is somehow off the beaten track offered him a great deal; the literature dealing with the right to the full return from labour, which in the period after Smith assumed a more and more 'professionally' economic form (compare Marx himself in *Theorien über den Mehrwert*, Vol. 1 on the development since Smith; A. Menger, loc. cit., and G. Alder, introduction to the fourth number of *Hauptwerke des Sozialismus und der Sozialpolitik*). Here also belong Ch. Hall, *The Effects of Civilization on the People in European States*, 1805, and furthermore, a number of authors in the second and third decade of the nineteenth century: Anon, *The Source and Remedy of the National Difficulties . . .*, 1821; P. Ravenstone, *Few Doubts as to the Correctness of Some Opinions . . .*, 1821; W. Thompson, *An Inquiry Into the Principles of the Distribution of Wealth Most Conducive to Human Happiness*, 1824 (in many respects Thompson was a successor of R. Owen, who also belongs here, but was in his economic theory much more profound than the latter); R. Hodgskin, *Popular Political Economy*, 1827, and other works; Bray, *Labour's Wrongs and Labour's Remedy*, 1839. In all these authors the labour theory of value assumes a particular meaning which we must not look for either in Smith or Ricardo: the significance of an ethical law and in addition the meaning which is even more important to us, that work creates value and is the only cause for the phenomenon of value. The reasons given for this are often faulty, often any attempt to give reasons at all is lacking—in fact it is an old idea which had been developed by many nations and it is not a scientific perception which suddenly breaks here into economic theory. This influence, at any rate, is the reason for a difference in the conceptions of the phenomenon of value held by Ricardo and Marx. Moreover, all these authors explain, with some occasional qualifications. interest and rent as wage robbery, even if this explanation assumes different forms. Marx does not adopt this idea. According to him, as according to Rodbertus, the worker receives in fact the value of his labour power. In spite of this, however, this idea contains the root of the conception of surplus value and surplus labour which Marx conceived and explained merely in a different form.

We find this idea also in St Simon, although Marx received a greater stimulus, even as regards the formulation of questions, from Proudhon whom he treated so badly. It is true that this economist cannot be rated very highly as a theorist. His *Système des contradictions économiques ou philosophie de la misère* (1846), his *Organisation du credit* (1848) and his *Interêt principal* (1850) are full of faulty observations and gross logical errors. Yet a connection between the two writers is unmistakable, and Marx' pamphlet directed against him, *Misère de la philosophie*, involves a great injustice. His proposition 'travailler c'est produire de rien' (in the *Solution du problème social*), his argument against the productivity of capital and land—that they do not produce anything without labour—led him directly to the conclusion that the landowners and capitalists appropriate without doing anything in return part of the product of labour, because the worker in his battle for wages receives as much as he could produce for himself, while all the surplus which must be ascribed to co-operation falls to the landlord and capitalist. This is not the argument used by Marx and is very inferior to the latter's argumentation, but is nevertheless a theory of surplus value in the sense in which it was formulated by Marx. Perhaps it did not serve as a starting point but it could easily have done so.

All this, however, merely refers to the theoretical foundations of Marx' thought. What he added resulted partly, as e.g. his theory of the reserve army from his criticism of what he found before him, and is in part quite independent. Above all, Marx is quite independent as regards the way in which he set his theory into the context of far-reaching sociological facts. Only in Germany was the success of Marx great and lasting. In England he found only a few followers who soon dispersed. (Most important work: Hyndman, *Economics of Socialism*, 1896.) In France and Italy his proper scientific performance had little effect, although his practical programme and some of his catchwords exercised some influence—even there he was, and still is, respected more as a sociologist than as an economist (compare for Italy: Michels, *Il Marxismo in Italia*, 1909; in some respects Loria can be described as a follower of Marx). The critical and apologetical literature of Marxism is very extensive, but only very few critics penetrate into the innermost recesses of his thought structure, while his defenders are more successful in this respect. As elsewhere, the interest in his political theses, in the basic tenor of his thought and also in his sociology produced in these countries also a diversion from purely economic theory.

Of works which were wholly or partially devoted to a criticism of Marx' theory we may mention the following: v. Böhm-Bawerk, *Zum Abschluss des Marxschen Systems* (Knies Festgabe, 1896) and in *Geschichte und Kritik der Kapitalzinstheorieen*, v. Bortkiewicz, *Wertrechnung und Preisrechnung im Marxschen System* (*Archiv für Sozialwissenschaft und Sozialpolitik*, 1906. *et seq.*) also in Conrad's *Jahrbuch*, third issue, Vol. 34; K. Diehl, *Sozialwissenschaftliche Erläuterugen . . .*, v. Komorzynski, in *Zeitschrift für Volkswirtschaft, Sozialpolitik und Verwaltung*, 1897, Lexis in Conrad's *Jahrbuch*, Vol. 2, Lange in Conrad's *Jahrbuch*, third issue, Vol. 14; Tugan-Baranowsky, *Theoretische Grundlagen des Marxismus*, 1905.

This also settles the problem of the relations between value (monetary expression of the quantity of labour inherent in a commodity) and price (monetary expression of exchange value) while taking into account the differences of the periods of production and in the composition of capital. It also settles the often treated problem of the 'discrepancy' or 'contradiction' between the first volume of *Das Kapital*, in which the former point of view prevails and the third volume in which the latter predominates. It might be assumed that no real contradiction exists either objectively or subjectively, although Marx may have had different ideas at different stages of his scientific journey, which indeed lasted a lifetime, about the extent of the distance between the original law of exchange and the actual determination of prices under capitalism. Incidentally, Ricardo proceeded quite similarly, since he also arrived gradually and under the influence of objections raised against him at a lower opinion of the correctness of the original law of exchange. This is revealed in the hardly noticeable yet very significant changes in the text of his first edition and also in his letters. Thus also the question is answered to what extent Marx ascribed to the original law of exchange an 'historical' significance—in fact exactly to the same extent as did Ricardo—and, furthermore, to what extent he regarded it merely as an abstraction. In details there are certainly differences between the two thinkers: Marx undertook to elaborate Ricardo's thought and to perfect it. He tried to give deeper reasons for the part played by labour and to analyse it—as by his distinction between labour power and labour product etc.—but this and other elements are of comparatively small importance.

Only on one point is there an essential difference between Marx and Ricardo. Ricardo states simply: If two entrepreneurs employ one hundred workers each during one year, one, in order to produce consumption goods, the other in order to manufacture a machine, and if in the second year the former does so again while the latter now in turn produces consumption goods with the machine which wears out in the process, the labour contained in the product of the two years is the same. Because, however, the former could sell his product of the first year at the end of it while the latter could not do so, it is obvious that the capital expended by the second entrepreneur during the first year must bear interest also during the second year; in consequence, the final product of the second entrepreneur must yield more than twice as much as does the yearly product of the former. With Marx, however, the machine does not automatically continue to bear interest during the second year, though the profit of the first year is already contained in its value. He starts, however, by asking himself the question how the constant capital acquires such a higher value; then he does not simply add this higher value to his 'labour value' but he investigates, keeping as his starting point the valuing principle which results from the original law of value, how the tendency towards an equalization of profits modifies this principle and distributes in our example the total profit of both entrepreneurs in such a way as to bring about equality in the rate of profit per unit of capital and time. To Ricardo, therefore, the unequal prolongation of the period of production as the result of the employment of constant capital appears simply as a cause of the deviation of prices from the law of labour value because of the need for the payment of more interest for capital that has been employed for a longer period. Marx, however, vigorously grasps the idea which is potentially contained in this argumentation and stresses the fact that this addition of interest is merely taken away from other capitalists by the operation of the law of the equal rate of profit. In the case of Ricardo, on the other hand, it was still possible to assume that the increased interest was added newly to the total amount of interest to be found in the economy. According to Marx, therefore, it is not the values that are changed by the tendency towards an equalization of profits, but merely the prices. The latter are in his view not merely expressions of the former; but the process by which prices are determined alters the results of the determination of values.

This theory of value which was formulated by Ricardo soon met with disapproval. Already at this period there developed a controversy on value in which above all Ricardo and De Quincey participated on one side and Bailey, Malthus and Say on the other. In this respect, therefore, the two 'tendencies', mentioned already, collided with each other for the first time. Two questions were involved in this situation. Firstly, the element of the value in use, which found its protagonists in Bailey and Say. Ricardo refuted this definition with the age old argument that it was proved irrelevant by the fact that very useful things were often quite valueless.[1] This argument established beyond a doubt the fact which is often denied even today that Ricardo—and even Cairnes in his controversy with Jevons—pushed aside the conception of value in use, not because it was 'self-evident' but because he could not see how it was possible to derive from it the exchange value. Say did not maintain this point of view very skilfully and did not grasp the essential point, yet he recognized the fundamental importance of the value in use and saw how impossible it is to consider the costs of production as the cause of the price.

Secondly, what was in question—particularly between Ricardo and Malthus—was the importance of supply and demand. Here, too, it is characteristic that what was decisive for Ricardo—and likewise later for Marx—was by no means the emptiness of the formula of supply and demand but the fact that at first he regarded it as incompatible with his own views. (Compare, e.g. *Letters to Malthus*, p. 148.) Nevertheless, the formula gained increasingly in influence, especially in connection with the theory of international values which altogether must be considered as a forerunner of later trends. This theory slowly emerged from the discussions on free trade. For a long time people had been content with the well-known general arguments in favour of free trade without investigating more deeply its effects on the system of value and price amongst the nations concerned. Thus we see that even Hume still does not clearly grasp the proposition that imports and exports mutually condition one another and must achieve some balance; nor did Smith attempt to grasp exactly the immediate advantages of international trade for the state of satisfaction amongst all concerned.

[1] The discrepancy between the amount of the exchange value of a commodity and its importance for welfare forms the essential *contradiction économique* of Proudhon. He believes that this contradiction was of necessity fatal to the capitalist economy. B. Hildebrand resolved this 'contradiction' rather neatly.

The decisive steps were taken only in later years: Foster's clear and final distinction between balance of trade and balance of payments, *Principle of Commercial Exchanges*, 1804, Torrens' formulation of the principle of an international division of labour and of the way in which total profits are distributed amongst the nations concerned, *The Economists Refuted*, 1808. It was to the credit of Ricardo that he elaborated the theory of international values and that he based it on the principle of comparative costs, because in doing so he once and for all created the theoretical equipment for an adequate treatment of this problem. Above all it was to his credit that he showed that even if one country is absolutely superior to another in all respects, the latter is not automatically ousted by competition but gains likewise a definite advantage. Ricardo also describes the corresponding monetary transaction in a manner which remained classical for a long time. His immediate successors did not add anything and even John Stuart Mill did not go materially beyond Ricardo; indeed his principal contribution is not particularly valuable and in some detailed points his presentation is less correct than that of Ricardo. Cherbuliez assumed a similarly high position. Hermann represented an advance because he showed in opposition to Nebenius that equality between the rates of profit in various countries could only be brought about by movements of capital, and because he applied some essential corrections to Ricardo's theory of the movements of money long before Goschen did so.

Another advance was made by Hagen who explains the fact, which people had always sensed but had never clearly understood before him, that low tariffs can bring profits to one of the countries concerned, even if the assumptions of the theory of free trade are accepted. We may also mention von Mangoldt's statement. A further advance is due to Cairnes, who applied the methods of the theory of international values also to the theory of national values, that is, to those cases where it is impossible to talk of completely free 'mobility' of capital and labour even within a country. The most modern statement of the classical theory of the matter is provided by Bastable, *Theory of International Trade*, 1903. We owe, as we may add at once, a number of new conclusions which cannot be enumerated here to Marshall (a privately printed memorandum, 1875, from which conclusions were printed in Pantaleoni's, *Teoria dell economia politica pura* and in Cunynghame's, *Geometrical Method of Political Economy*, 1904). We are also indebted to Auspitz and Lieben, *Untersuchungen über die Theorie desPreises*, 1888, and above all to Edgeworth, *Economic Journal*, 1894, Cournot, *Principes mathématiques de la theorie des richesses*, 1836, and Sidgwick[1] undertook two original but not altogether successful attempts to improve on the theory.

The importance of this theory for the doctrines of value and price consisted in the fact that as regards the determination of international values any other determining cause except the intensity of the reciprocal demand is completely lacking; nevertheless even here 'natural' or equilibrium prices result. This theory, if thought out consistently and if its basic conception was thoroughly grasped, was bound to draw attention to the unsatisfactory character of Ricardo's approach. It was John Stuart Mill who took the decisive step in a new direction. He recognized first of all that the kind of price determination which is described by the formula of supply and demand is of general validity and contains the original law of exchange as a special case. Then he limited the latter—completely changing its real meaning—by stressing one important element, namely that of labour cost, and in doing so he allowed the element of the quantity of labour to recede in favour of the element of the actual rate of wages. Finally, he put the point of view of the entrepreneur into the foreground in dealing with the cost of production, so that in his treatment the labour theory of value and price joined with the theory of the costs of production; in other words he produced a point of view the inadequate character of which had induced Ricardo to undertake his whole analysis.

[1] Bastiat was one of the most energetic protagonists of free trade but did not add anything to its theory. Friedrich List, however, with his argument of the 'educative tariff' at least secured recognition in the science of economics for a popular slogan of the day. We meet the latter in consequence also in John Stuart Mill and Du Mesnil-Mavigny (*L'Economie politique devenue science exacte*, 1859). In the latter there appear also List's ideas of the necessity for a national economy which corresponds to the physical and social conditions prevailing in the life of the nation.

Of course the cost of production theory was now no more tenable than it has been at an earlier period: now it merely signified that Ricardo's basic conception had been abandoned, and for the rest it constituted a kind of intermediate position which could not be maintained in the long run. One further step was bound to lead to the utility theory of prices, and those authors who later attacked the utility theory of value from the point of view of this variant of the cost of production theory were soon forced to realize that their position was untenable. The other alternative was the attempt to look in the empirically given amount of the cost of production for an element that was independent of the utility value. This way, too, was taken and it led to the only cost theory which was held even after Mill by authors of rank, a theory which bases the phenomenon of cost on the element of the disutility of labour and of abstention from enjoyment.[1] We shall have to return to this point.

11. As has already been pointed out the theory of distribution was for the classical economists by far the most important problem. They were concerned with the proportional distribution of a social product which otherwise was considered as given and the *absolute* size of which together with its *absolute* changes were taken into account only in passing—and almost never as dependent also on the manner in which distribution was carried out. In order to understand the extent of the progress made we must take Smith's theory of distribution with all its popular superficiality as an example. We can do this only very broadly and turn to the theories of the three, or, as the case may be, four branches of income,

[1] We should really mention still other theories of cost in view of the fact that an essential part of the picture of economic reality depends on its author's attitude to the phenomenon of cost. We must, however, limit ourselves. The costs of reproduction theory (Carey, Ferrara, Dühring) would have to be mentioned amongst others. Strictly speaking it meant little more than the fact that in it an element has been stressed that is common to all cost theories: What is certainly decisive for the exchange value are never the costs expended but those that must be expended in case of further production. Nevertheless, the cost of reproduction theory led to some special results. Bastiat, moreover, replaced the element of the costs expended by the element of the costs of production saved by the purchaser. These saved costs in his case measure the 'service' rendered to the purchaser.

although in doing so we obliterate certain individual basic features.

In the theory of rent we find at first still some traces of the old popular belief that the ground-rent simply results from the fact that things grow on the land, that in fact it is a 'Gift of Nature'. This was taught by Malthus, who in other respects assumes quite a different point of view (*An Inquiry Into the Nature and Progress of Rent*, 1815).[1] Already Smith, however, made a real attempt to explain matters with the idea that land is not a product and in consequence has no costs of production; therefore, the fact that products of the land have a price can be explained only by a 'monopoly in land'. Th. P. Thompson[2], is the best representative of this idea, which, though it was merely based on an insufficient understanding of the nature of monopoly, makes itself often felt in the classical literature, as, e.g., in Senior and has a great many representatives even today. A third theory of rent advances the general theory of 'productive services' and must accordingly be associated in the first place with the name of Say. Here also belongs Hermann whose conception of all material goods of production as a fund the use of which is transmitted to the products without its substance being used up, so that the prices paid for the uses to which it is put form a net income, proved its worth especially in the theory of the ground-rent. In combining rent and interest as substantially identical and different merely in the form in which they are calculated, Hermann is the forerunner of a great many later thinkers amongst whom we may mention several modern Americans (Clark, Fisher, Fetter).

This theory, which gained in influence the more people learned to appreciate a genuine explanation of the nature of the various branches of income as opposed to their mere size and the more they demanded a uniform theory of distribution, explains ground-rent like all other forms of income as the result of the purely economic role played by the factor land in production. A fourth

[1] He adds still another explanatory reason: Agricultural production creates as it were its own demand, since every extension produces an increase in population—an entirely fallacious idea which indeed fell to the ground.

[2] Th. P. Thompson, *The True Theory of Rent*, 1826. The merit of this work rests on its criticism of Ricardo.

theory proceeded differently. It was held by authors who likewise took the conception of productive services as their basis but in the case of ground-rent substituted for the 'service' rendered by land an alleged expenditure of capital and labour by the landlord, so that ground-rent appeared as interest and wages. This theory was held by Carey and under his influence by Ferrara.[1] Much more important, however, is the theory which was first formulated by Anderson (1777) and then by West (1815) and Malthus (1815) but was recognized in its full significance by Ricardo from whom Thünen took it over—the differential theory of rent. In its deepest meaning it represents the reverse side of Ricardo's theory of value.

It purports to answer the question: How can the quantity of labour be an index of exchange relations if in the commodities there are contained unequal 'units of land'? People answered this question by establishing first of all the validity of the law of exchange for the products that were produced on land which bears no rent because it is the worst and is considered as a free commodity; then by proving that the labour which is required for their production must generally determine their price, since they would not be produced for a lower price, while at the same time equal quantities of the same commodity cannot have different prices. This is the reason why the exchange values of all quantities of products that had been produced under other conditions than the most unfavourable ones must contain a surplus above the quantity given in the labour index and to this extent deviate indeed from the original law of exchange. This deviation, however, does not nullify the latter because the exchange value of products of the land remains nevertheless proportional to the quantity of labour contained in part of them. Furthermore, this deviation does not influence wages and profits because competition among workers and capitalists makes this surplus flow into the pockets of the landlords. Accordingly, what looked like a real refutation of the law of exchange cannot only be made innocuous but can even be employed to advantage, even if only with the help of a special factor, the law of diminish-

[1] Bastiat's attitude to the problem of ground-rent can most probably be characterized best by the statement that he altogether denies the existence of a *pure* ground-rent.

ing returns on land.

Three cases of rent were differentiated at once: the rent derived from land of higher fertility, the rent of intra-marginal expenditure (dose) of labour and capital—that is the last expenditure which precedes the one which is economically just possible—and the rent of location which was especially stressed by Thünen, though it was already known to Ricardo. This latter rent, which constituted a first attempt at applying in general the law of diminishing returns on land, was later on also used for the treatment of urban ground-rents. In judging this theory we have to distinguish four points: its absolute cognitive value, its importance to the classical system, its historical importance for the development of economic thought, and the value of individual perceptions which the classical economists derived from it, or at least stated in this guise. The absolute cognitive value of this theory is small, not only because several well-founded objections—and some unfounded ones (Carey)—emerged at once and because a discussion which has continued to this day brought to light some serious defects, but most of all because it really explains nothing. It is a purely formal contrivance in order to extirpate rent from the process of exchange. Probably this was precisely what Ricardo intended. Yet as such it was of fundamental importance to the classical economists. When J. Mill, Senior, McCulloch and others deal with the problem of distribution they stress again and again with satisfaction the fact that rent is being eliminated in the process of distribution, that it is 'extraneous' or 'extrinsic' to it, etc., so that the salient point was merely the way in which wages and profits were distributed. For the development of the science of economics this theory of rent provided for a long time a firm guiding line and in so far as its representatives conceded points a theme for discussions in the course of which many a point was clarified. As regards the fourth point mentioned above it was in the special case of rent that the classical economists first recognized with conceptual clarity the fact that incomes are strictly speaking never the cause but always merely the consequence of the prices of products[1] and that even

[1] This conception was later applied in a more generalized form. But before this was done consistently many authors distinguished between elements of

if the former entirely disappeared the latter would be influenced only in a secondary manner. Apart from this there was still a lot of practical insight and correct observation that was connected with the incomplete structure of this theory.

Let us now mention some of the most important further developments of the Ricardian ground-rent theory—for in spite of all doubts it deserves to be called that. Above all the pattern of this theory, the description of yields as surpluses over and above a marginal yield, was generally applied. Just as according to Ricardo still further doses of capital and labour were progressively applied to the given piece of land, we can easily conceive without having to stretch our imagination too far that equal doses of labour and land are progressively applied to a given amount of capital and that equal doses of capital and land are progressively handed over to a given number of workers, so that in consequence interest on capital and wages appear in the form of rent. Of course it is just the possibility of this generalization which reveals the small value of the whole approach as a special theory of ground-rent, but this does not alter the fact that this approach proved fruitful for certain purposes. In the field of the history of economic doctrines it is especially interesting as one of the ways which were bound to lead from the classical system to different points of view.[1] Furthermore, the law of diminishing returns in agricultural production was soon enlarged into a law of diminishing returns from production as such, and phenomena which were quite analogous to ground-rent were discovered in the field of industry. As an example we may mention Mangoldt's bold conception of a general rent as the consequence of the inequality of the conditions of production; there are in fact innumerable traces of this point of view.

The element of the gift of nature was stressed in the conception of rent, and in consequence elements of rent were found also in the wages of especially capable intellectual or manual labour power. The factor of missing costs was likewise put forward and wherever

[1] This line was taken by American writers under the leadership of John B. Clark.

income 'that determined prices' from those 'that were determined by prices' —not a very brilliant intermediate position.

a great expenditure has to be made for a longer period, which once made cannot be withdrawn again, it was assumed that this factor applied by way of analogy. From this sprang the conception of the quasi-rent (Marshall) and the perception that according to the length of time under consideration the range of yields that behave like such 'rents' changes, so that under one point of view almost nothing, not even cultivable land, yields profits of a rent character, while under a different point of view almost everything does so.

The ground-rent theories of Marx and Rodbertus differ considerably from that of Ricardo and from each other. Nevertheless all three have one feature in common—the competition amongst the workers and capitalists secure an income to the landowners, amongst whom competition has a less severe effect owing to the fact that land cannot be increased. In Marx as well as in Rodbertus there exists not only a 'differential' but also an 'absolute' ground-rent.[1] This rent is part of the surplus value which is inherently uniform or, as the case may be, it is part of the rent of ownership which is also inherently uniform. Marx' idea amounts to the following: In agriculture comparatively little constant capital is employed, in consequence the proportion of surplus value to capital value is great. While, however, in industry, owing to the prevailing competition and because of the validity of the law of exchange resulting from this competition, no producer derives an advantage from employing less constant capital than does another, in agriculture he would have such an advantage, because here competition is limited by the condition of the possession of land. He must, however, obviously cede the advantage to the landlord—hence the ground-rent. Rodbertus does not base his otherwise quite similar argumentation on the—alleged or real—fact of a small proportion of constant capital but—most unfortunately—on the fact that the agricultural in contrast to the industrial producer does not have to pay for material (raw material), or at least not so much, because his most important material is the soil given by nature. Hence a

[1] Attempts have been made to find an absolute ground-rent also in Ricardo, but the entire plan of his system is based on the exclusive existence of a differential rent. Even if Ricardo occasionally made statements which point to an absolute ground-rent he set no store by it and never used it theoretically.

surplus profit, the ground-rent.[1]

As has already been pointed out, the limitation which appears so desirable to many economists by which distribution is confined only to two categories of participants in the economic process,[2] can be achieved in two ways: by the elimination of the ground-rent according to Ricardo's example or by including it in a wider conception of rent which comprises yields from capital as well as from land, as Hermann, Marx and Rodbertus did, each in his own manner. Once this is done it is possible either to explain wages and profits *pari passu* as based on the same principle or on different ones, and thus to establish the relative size of both, or to adopt the attitude that, as their total amount is in fact given, all that would be necessary would be to ascertain amount and operational rules for one of the two. This latter point of view is that of Ricardo. In his thought the following argument emerged with full clarity from a maze of qualifications and contradictions: the worker is the 'producer' of the total product from which possibly the ground-rent is taken away in advance. The exchange value of each product is approximately and on the whole proportional to the quantity of labour contained in it. What remains of it in the hands of the 'capitalist', and therefore becomes profit, depends on how much the capitalist has to give to the 'producer'. It depends further on the quantity of labour—in relation to which the exchange value of the 'wage goods' is taken into account proportionately—which is contained in the quantities of those goods which finally fall to the share of the producer. From this the rate of profit also results and for the latter the following proposition emerges: profit is essentially determined by the real value of wages; it rises when the latter falls and vice versa.

For a better understanding of this famous theorem we may further add that it refers merely to the relation of values according to the index of labour value; the supply of goods for the capitalist

[1] We cannot enter into a more detailed discussion of this theme. Compare the excellent study by v. Bortkiewicz in *Archiv für die Geschichte des Sozialismus und der Arbeiterbewegung*, Vol. 1, and the works by Alder, Lexis, Schippel and Zuns mentioned therein.

[2] Translator's footnote: There is no exact English equivalent for *Wirtschaftsubjekt*.

can rise simultaneously with that for the workers and likewise profits and wages can rise and fall together according to a different index of value. Ricardo, furthermore, by no means overlooks the influence of productivity of labour and of the length of the period of production on profits; only he does not see in them essential factors which determine the great historical movement of profits. Finally, the theorem does not rest on the assumption of constant prices of products, as many critics have assumed.

From this it immediately follows that changes in wages do not affect prices or do so only as far as the equality of the rate of profit in conjunction with the inequality of the organic composition of capital renders this necessary. It follows further that even if prices were affected this would not influence the rate of profit. Changes in the conditions of production of other commodities than those consumed by the workers do not affect the rate of profit either, since expenditure and return merely are changed in an equal manner. On the other hand changes in the conditions of production of 'wage goods' do in fact occasion some changes in wages and can thus influence the rate of profit. Ricardo was of the opinion that this was so in most cases. Amongst the wage goods there is especially one, the production of which can occasionally be increased as the result of advance in production and as the result of imports without an increase in the costs per unit or even with lower costs per unit, although in the course of events over a period of history it can only be increased by constantly increasing the expenditure per unit of production: this commodity is corn. Since corn, and in fact all foodstuffs in consequence will progressively rise in price if population and capital increase, the rate of profit will fall progressively—this indeed explains its decrease in history. Simultaneously the ground-rent is bound to rise progressively, but while the worker derives no advantage from the rise in his wages because he cannot buy any more corn for himself than before, the position of the landlord is more favourable,[1] because now more corn falls to his share and this corn has in addition a higher value. This then is Ricardo's famous theory of the evolutionary trends

[1] And more unfavourable in the case of advances in production.

of distribution,[1] which he published in the same year, *Essay on the Influence of a Low Price of Corn on the Profits of Stock*, 1815, as West published his and which he elaborated in his *Principles* with a small modification. We should admire its ingenious conception but should also note that he constantly introduced in the course of his argument new assumptions, new facts and concrete correlations, which in reality are only effective in conjunction with many others, and made them the basis for further arguments.

Especially those final conclusions which are practically most important and which purport to illuminate economic activities throughout the centuries are by no means the logical conclusions which had been derived from a basic theory but are in fact derived from a basic conception into which quite concrete data have been incorporated. This constant process of premising concrete data, this limitation of the investigation to individual cases selected out of several theoretically possible ones, this belief in large cross-sections and this neglect of detailed theoretical work constitute both the strength and the weakness of this argument: they make possible precise and forceful conclusions but they also involve the danger that people might arrive at a caricature of reality without making any real logical mistakes and even more that people might forget how uncertain and 'approximative' the conclusions in fact are, even though they may be practically very relevant.

Ricardo, therefore, as it were, touched reality in its fullness with his finger but only at some of its points. If he had detached himself more from it he would have had a more comprehensive view of it. The rigid chains of cause and effect with which he tried to connect facts, between which a mutual relation indeed exists, are often unreliable and while some of Ricardo's assertions refer to the immediate present, others refer to an infinitely distant future.

In consequence that characteristically unfair criticism which can be observed so often in our discipline was by no means required in order to discover that Ricardo was full of contradictions and difficult to understand. Even his immediate pupils did not under-

[1] This theory was opposed by Carey and Bastiat with different conceptions which we cannot go into. Rodbertus' 'law of the decreasing wage quota' also can merely be mentioned.

stand him and already James Mill and McCulloch spoiled his theorems of profit and made them trite. Although we continue to find traces of his point of view in scientific works and thoughtless repetitions and 'refutations' of his trenchantly formulated conclusions in popular works, even John Stuart Mill's contribution (*Essays on Some Unsettled Questions of Political Economy*, 1841, No. 4, and *Principles*) places Ricardo's thought as it were on a soft bed, in order to let it die gently. All authors of this school, however, clung to the explanation of the decline in the rate of profit, as it was provided by Ricardo and West, and rejected most emphatically the old explanation as formulated by Smith according to which the increase in capital intensified competition between the capitalists and thus depressed profits, because competition merely influenced the prices of products and a general fall of all prices could have no influence on the rate of profit.

The point of view, however, that profit is merely a residue and can only be explained because for some reason labour which produces the entire product uniformly only receives part of the profit is certainly in keeping with Ricardo's pattern of thought, even if he himself does not express it but occasionally makes statements which point in a difterent direction. This point of view was not adopted by the authors of this school who tried to follow Ricardo when he made those hints in a different direction. Yet they certainly did not overlook this train of thought. Thus the younger Mill (*Principles*, book II, ch. XV, para 5) says: 'The cause of profit is that labour produces more than is required for its support.' In this proposition Mill hints at the 'physical productivity' of labour which corresponds to the productivity of the soil. We have met this proposition already as the first and most primitive theory of ground-rent. The theorem also corresponds to the physical productivity of capital which we are going to meet as basis for the most primitive theory of interest. Mill, however, saw obviously that this element explains in fact nothing at all and accordingly he does not base his own theory of interest on it, in spite of the word 'cause' which here is quite out of place and should be replaced by 'condition'.

Marx, on the other hand, made use of this idea. His theory of surplus value and of exploitation is undoubtedly based on one of Ricardo's suggestions, which was probably unintentional. Rodbertus also made use of it though in a somewhat different manner. There were other stimuli in this direction as well. It was only Ricardo, however, who provided a scientific basis for Marx whose theory of surplus value can be considered as a logical development of this basis in one direction. Ricardo preceded Marx in applying the original law of exchange to labour—according to Marx to the commodity called labour force—and, which is decisive, formulated precisely and placed into the centre of his argument the difference between the quantity of labour contained in wages and that contained in the total product. This difference is the surplus value. Already from Ricardo's point of view it would be possible to say that it owes its origin to unpaid labour power. Marx formulated and elaborated this point of view still more neatly. He distinguished between surplus value and profit, at least more clearly—in our opinion he did so for the first time. Like Rodbertus he comprised in one category all manifestations of surpluses over wages which according to this point of view must be considered as essentially identical. Finally, through his analysis of capital he arrived at the proposition that the origin of surplus value is not due to capital in its entirety but merely to variable capital and that a part of the surplus value accrues to constant capital merely through the action of competition.[1] From this resulted for him a different explanation for the fall of the rate of profit. Production in which constant capital is employed is distinguished from production in which this is not the case merely by its duration and its productivity, because, if the former did not require more time and did not produce more goods than the latter, it would be quite irrelevant whether the goods had been produced directly or by the detour of a preceding production of tools. The greater productivity is relevant for the rate of profit only inasmuch as it presses down the exchange value of wage goods, but we can completely disregard this factor in this context since corn plays a decisive part in the complex of

[1] In these propositions there is contained Marx' theory of exploitation which we cannot consider here more closely any more than other characteristic features of this system.

wage goods for which, according to the views of this entire school, an increase in productivity comes into the question only temporarily.

The extension of the period of time of production, however, has as its consequence that the same amount of surplus value must now be distributed over a longer period of time—hence the decline in the rate of profit. This, however, would merely constitute an additional reason for the decline since the one given by Ricardo—the decrease of the rate of surplus value in the case of the increase of the labour quantity required for the production of wage goods—is not really affected by it. This new treatment of the factor of time furthermore induces Marx to deny the existence of an antagonism between profit and wages and to refute the assertion that profit is not influenced by changes in the conditions of production except in the case of wage goods. Yet this argument also merely adds one other new factor which would not prejudice the importance of Ricardo's view for an understanding of the tendencies in the development of the rate of surplus value and even, if we introduce certain relevant assumptions, of the rate of profit.

Let us now briefly survey the theory of wages and interest of the period. As Cannan (*loc. cit.*, p. 200) rightly remarks, at the beginning of this period it did not at all appear as a problem why the worker receives his wages. He produced indeed the whole product and what was problematic was merely why it did not fall to his share entirely. In consequence, it was not the character of wages but merely their level that was a subject for debate. There were only slight suggestions of the conception of a distinguishable share in the total product for the worker in return for his performance and, with it, of an attempt to explain wages in this way and to make the correlation between the price of the product and wages a basis for a theory of wages. Examples for this line of thought can be found in Say and his successors, then in M. Longfield, *Lectures on Political Theory*, 1834, and also to some extent in Malthus, but above all in Hermann and Thünen who grasped the conception of the product of the marginal worker with complete clarity. For the others it was merely necessary to look for the concrete external circumstances which prevent wages from absorbing the total product as they had done in primitive circumstances.

The view that the ordinary manual worker earns approximately his livelihood and that this is inevitable was of ancient origin. We find it as early as in the seventeenth century, later also in the Physiocrats and in Turgot. Adam Smith propounds it likewise, even if with some careful qualifications and with the wealth of individual observations and statements which we have come to expect of him. In this case, too, their common sense conceals the lack of depth in his basic assumptions, amongst which the differentiation between high wages and expensive labour is the most important. If we wish to find a genuine theory of wages in his writings this could merely be a residual theory: the worker who confronts landlord and capitalist must give part of his product to them; what remains constitutes his wages. Nothing is further from his mind than the thought that if the worker were at the same time also landlord and capitalist he would indeed receive the whole product but not as wages. The idea also, which forms the starting point for a comprehension of the capitalist process of distribution, namely, that wages are a price, is pursued by him without much energy. It is only in the later chapters of the *Wealth* that demand for labour and the price of food appear as factors which determine wages, while in subsequent years people proceeded precisely from these two factors.

The demand for labour was based on capital and under the influence of Malthus' essay it was assumed that this demand was confronted by a supply which tends to increase. In this connection we find already in Ricardo a tendency to assume that the working population increases faster than capital, and in James Mill and McCulloch an attempt to prove that this was necessary if a nation not living in a new country allowed its physical power of reproduction to operate unchecked. Since they, however, do not assert that this does in fact happen and since they in following Torrens' example replace the physical subsistence level by a customary standard of life which varies according to time and place, there can be no question of the alleged 'pessimism' of Ricardo, Malthus and their successors. Nor can there be any question of some callousness of feeling which, incidentally, would be scientifically quite irrelevant. It is incomprehensible how anybody who has read the chapters on wages of Ricardo and Malthus can talk of pessimism or callousness. For the rest the historical spirit of both chapters—not only that of Malthus—is remarkable. One could not have found a worse expression for Ricardo's views than that of the 'brazen law of wages', though at the same time none more suitable for the agitator. In particular he referred expressly to the possibility of reaching and maintaining a high standard which was incapable of being limited rigidly. It is true that if the population increases faster than capital, wages are bound to fall. If, however, at the same time the prices of the wage goods rise this will counteract the tendency mentioned, if customary standards are depressed in consequence, because in this case the increase in the population would cease.

A little later people began to call that part of the annual social product which is used for the payment of wages for workers engaged in production the wage fund and to define the latter more precisely as a quantitative expression of the effective demand for labour as its exists at each particular moment. It was assumed that it was possible to master the causes which determine the supply of labour. If in addition people were to succeed in finding firm causes which determine this part of the social product (the wage fund) they would have arrived at the wages of the ordinary manual worker. This could be done without difficulties if there were no different types of labour, and with certain but not insurmountable difficulties, if differences in quality had to be taken into consideration. The role played by the physical power of reproduction for the supply of labour was assigned to saving as regards the demand for labour, because the wage fund mentioned consists either of goods which replaced others, that served for the payment of wages in former periods, or of *new* wage goods. In the first case the fund owes its origin to former savings as understood by the classical economists, in the latter it has been increased by recent savings.

In consequence, nothing can be used for the payment of wages that has not been saved beforehand by the capitalist through whose hand it is bound to pass, that is, that has been designated by him for 'reproductive' consumption instead of for his own.[1] While, therefore, there exists a direct relation between that part of the social production that has been saved and wages, there exists merely an indirect relation between the whole social product and wages, namely as far as the total size of the social product influences savings. Immediately after Ricardo and up to the time of John Stuart Mill the indirect relation was neglected while the main emphasis was placed on the direct relation and this is characteristic of the well-known wage fund theory.[2] From this in turn there follows the tendency, so characteristic of the classical economists also in other respects, to sever the connection between wages and labour output. In addition the proposition emerges that the workers, whatever their number may be and whatever they might try to achieve by strikes and organization, must always share the same total amount of wages. It also follows, however, that the entrepreneurs cannot depress wages below the level mentioned above, unless they save less.

Behind this entire argument there lies the view that in each period of production wages are advanced to the workers out of the capital of the entrepreneur. The wage fund theory suffers from the same weakness which we can often observe in the classical writers in other respects: it isolates one link in the chain of economic connections—in this case capital—and accords to it a causal function which it does not possess in this neat way, since in its turn it is itself determined by other links. Yet with this qualification the theory is not simply wrong, and there is a wealth of correct perceptions associated with it. In particular, although it is not true that a greater number of workers must share the same wage fund as a smaller number, it is correct that if the number of workers increases while the methods of production remain the same, the level of wages cannot increase proportionally but only to a lesser extent.

Furthermore, although the wage fund theory is a primitive and

[1] Mill's definition of savings as a productive spending has evoked unjustified protests, as, e.g. on the part of Jevons.

[2] As typical representatives J. Mill and McCulloch may be mentioned while Senior was more critical. Comp. McCulloch, *Treatise on Wages*, 1854.

incomplete instrument, it is quite useful in demonstrating some essential objective factors determining the level of wages and in establishing many relations of these factors with others in the economy. In all it is a good example of the whole tenor of the classical arguments, both as regards their bad and their good points. The external fate of this theory revealed some of the most dramatic aspects which our discipline can record. Celebrated by some as a great discovery and as an expression of deep wisdom, condemned by others as a bourgeois trick and as complete nonsense—misunderstood by both parties and exploited by them for political purposes—it became widely famous and notorious, and in this process its good points became more and more blurred, while its bad points were exaggerated into grotesque dimensions. From the point of view of the wage theory which we mentioned first, especially from that of Say and Thünen, it could have been supplemented and corrected, but nobody was interested in doing this. Only two writers, von Hermann and Longe, *A Refutation of the Wage-Fund Theory*, 1886, discussed the theory seriously but in such a hostile spirit, that it did not at all occur to them that strictly speaking they would have to put in its place propositions which were quite similar to those that seemed so objectionable to them in the wage fund theory. This attack remained almost completely unnoticed.

The popular attacks were mostly directed against the conception of the food of the workers as 'capital' which seemed to imply a degradation of the worker into a machine. These attacks signified little, although they played a part even in scientific literature. In 1869 there appeared a most unimportant book which repeated Longe's arguments in a verbose and incomplete manner: *On Labour*, by W. T. Thornton. John Stuart Mill in his review (*Fortnightly Review*, 1869) completely agreed with the author and declared, after having summarized the wage fund theory in the most unfavourable manner possible, that it was untenable—without giving any adequate reasons.[1] The astonishment was great and how-

[1] Yet even if this review was no great scientific achievement, it is all the same very characteristic of Mill's sympathies: with a sigh of relief he throws off the wage-fund theory in the way in which one delivers oneself of a

ever dominating Mill's influence was in English economics, many authors still clung to the wage-fund theory—as did for instance Cairnes, who attempted to formulate it in a better way. Yet the number of the faithful who followed the leader without asking why was great enough to destroy the wage fund theory. H. Sidgwick, F. A. Walker and others then dealt it the final blow. The general public, however, in whose face Mill had abjured the theory, naturally from now on passed on to the order of the day as far as it was concerned and saw in the whole business a fatal defeat for 'orthodox' economics at a time when the latter already began to lose ground. All this—what an insight into the forces that operate in our discipline!—without even a single argument having really successfully attacked the essence of the doctrine in a decisive manner. As was to be expected there emerged on the other side of the wave-like movement again elements of the wage-fund theory and today a more correct interpretation has begun to make itself felt.[1]

As regards the theory of interest[2] people went at first only slowly beyond the conception which had at last become dominant in the second half of the eighteenth century, according to which interest must be explained not by reference to money but to the determination of the value of goods. To this conception people clung in subsequent years. What was altogether decisive was the whole design within the classical picture of the economic process and in particular the physiocratic idea which Smith had introduced into English economics that capital is a part of the social product which sets labour in motion in various ways and advances their subsistence and tools. Adam Smith did not have a genuine theory of

[1] Compare Taussig, *The Wages Question*, 1892; Spiethoff in: *die Entwicklung der Volkswirtschaftslehre in Deutschland im XIX Jahrhundert*. (Schmollers Festgabe.)

[2] Compare v. Böhm-Bawerk, loc. cit.

burden borne reluctantly. Here we see clearly how little it was political desire that had made him cling to it, we see that he had stated the theory merely because he respected truth more than his political wishes, for there was no other proposition of the 'classics' that was more closely connected with a political slogan. If he had sympathized with this slogan this would have become apparent on this occasion, but the opposite emerged.

interest. His statements first of all reveal that trend towards the theory of exploitation which must always be the consequence of the conception that the worker produces the whole product and as a poor devil fares badly in selling his labour power, so that there remains a surplus for the employer. This, however, has nothing to do with the theory of exploitation in Marx' sense. Other theories as well can be found in his statements, either explicitly—such as the view that profit is an addition to price—or implicitly—such as the elements of the theory of productivity. As has already been mentioned, things were similar with Ricardo, only he offers the basis for a genuine Marxist theory of exploitation, which in a manner quite different from that of Smith explains profits as resulting from the conditions of work, and in connection with them, from the discrepancy between the labour value of the labour power and the labour value of the product of the worker. Besides, he clearly indicates a theory of abstention—those commodities the production of which requires some time must be worth more than those which can be produced with an equal quantity of labour in a shorter period of time, since the capitalist must wait longer for his returns.

Ricardo also indicated a theory of productivity—the rate of profit is determined by the yield of that unit of capital which has been applied last, that is, that amount of capital which has been applied to land bearing no rent. This latter idea was seized upon and elaborated by v. Thünen. Yet, however significant this view was, the whole train of thought on which it was materially based was really quite alien to Ricardo; it had in fact been developed already before Thünen did so, e.g. by Lauderdale, Say and Malthus who explain interest by the 'productive power of capital or by its 'productive services'. These writers, and in particular Lauderdale, deserve credit for having deliberately inquired into the cause and nature of interest, or better, for having persevered with their study of it. This question had indeed been asked already at an earlier period but had been in danger of being completely pushed into the background and only now a serious attempt was made to answer it. It is true that Lauderdale and his associates contented themselves with the proof that it was possible to produce more goods with machines—or the same number with smaller costs—than without them. This is inadequate for two reasons: first, this 'physical productivity' proves nothing for 'value productivity' and second, since machines are products of labour, labour would produce higher exchange values if employed in one way than it would do if it was employed otherwise for a similar period. This state of affairs could not last, or if it did, it would require a further explanation. This does not alter the fact that from an historical point of view this conception represented a great advance. A similar statement can be made about the use theory which was associated with the name of Hermann and was later put forward particularly by Menger and Knies. Its basic ideas is that there is something in capital which is not used up but provides again and again new 'uses', although most capital goods—all in fact except land—are economically absorbed by the products. It is certain that this idea is exposed to all the objections raised by Böhm-Bawerk against it,[1] yet it contains a good deal of insight. Apart from this all the representatives of this 'use theory' have contributed a considerable amount of detailed work towards a classification of the problem. This is especially true of Hermann, whose pronouncements on the rate of profit are amongst the best performances of the period. Neither the theory of productivity nor the use theory are accepted today in their pure form but many modern ideas are derived from them.

Yet even the immediate successors of Ricardo—we are no longer talking of the theory of exploitation—felt the need for a genuine theory of interest which offers more than a reference to a residual quantity. That we are right when we maintain that Ricardo offers indeed no explanation of the phenomenon of interest is proved by the desperate attempts on the part of J. Mill and McCulloch to produce such an explanation. If Ricardo had had definite views on this subject he would have communicated them to his pupils and would have preserved them from seeking in interest merely the wages for the labour embodied in the capital goods—thus J. Mill—or even the wages for fictitious labour which the commodities themselves, e.g. wine in a cellar, are supposed to perform over

[1] In *Kapital und Kapitalzins*, 1884.

and above the labour contained in them. (McCulloch.) This sort of thing could not be maintained for long.

The English theory of interest *par excellence*—in contrast to the predominantly Continental theory of productivity and use—was created by Senior. The idea that interest is a compensation for saving was bound to suggest itself to anybody who explains capital formation by saving. Hints in this direction are numerous. Hasbach, *Schmollers Jahrbuch*, 1905, drew our attention to a particularly explicit one, Germain Garnier, *Abrégé élémentaire des principes d'économie politique*, 1796. P. Scrope also, *Principles of Political Economy*, 1833 must be considered. Senior, however, did not merely propagate a catchphrase but gave to this theory a firmer basis by introducing the conception of 'abstinence'—later improved to 'waiting' or deferment of enjoyment—as a third factor of production. In connection with this he carried out extremely valuable investigations into the problems of interest and wages. This is also the theory of John Stuart Mill and Sidgwick.

When later on the cost theory confined itself to a psychological analysis of the phenomenon of cost, the element of the temporary abstinence from enjoyment was placed alongside the element of disutility (irksomeness) of labour; in the purest and most consistent manner by Cairnes. Furthermore, when the argument which is contained in the joke of the abstemious millionaire made itself felt, the theory was more precisely formulated by making the rate of interest dependent on the 'abstinence' of just that saver who is so poor that he would fall out if the rate of interest were to fall. In this form this theory has prevailed in England, either in its pure form or with certain admixtures, to this very day. It has had less success on the Continent, mostly in Italy. In the second half of the nineteenth century it gained supporters also in America.

For the reason already quoted a genuine theory of the profit of the entrepreneur could not develop at first. It is true that profit and interest on loans had already been distinguished in the eighteenth century but only in the sense that interest on loans was a profit paid to the capitalist who loans his capital. As usual we find already in Smith an indication of almost all the elements which became important later on, but it was Say who first attempted to explain the profit of the entrepreneur and his role in the economy by reference to his functions. The school of Ricardo achieved next to nothing in this matter and only in John Stuart Mill do we find more, probably under French influence. The best performance must, however, be attributed to v. Hermann and Mangoldt. About the middle of the century those conceptions were evolved which are expounded even today: the conception of the profit of the entrepreneur as wages of management, as a premium for risks taken (this view became fashionable especially in France), as a rent of ability (v. Mangoldt, then in America F. Walker) and as chance gain. Except in the case of the two German authors mentioned above this problem assumed merely a secondary place and resulted nowhere in more profound discussions. People saw in capital, as after all they still do today, so much the factor which creates or at least appropriates surplus value that there remained little space for the profit of the entrepreneur: This was the case particularly since the function of the entrepreneur was analysed so incompletely that in many cases all he was made to do was to pocket the profit.

12. Within the framework of this study it is impossible for us to describe specialized themes in detail. Thus we may merely mention the fact that during this epoch a special theory of monopoly was not evolved (Senior could be mentioned here rather than anybody else). This produced unfortunate consequences with regard to many of the problems and led to a completely unjustifiable misuse of the term monopoly. The theory of money, in the form in which we find it in Smith and as it prevailed during this period, consists in the idea of the material value of money. Apart from this we find some discussions of the function of money and of the qualities which predestine some commodities to a monetary role. The value of money can be explained by the value of the material of which it consists; unredeemable paper money or undervalued money is little more than a fraud. In addition we can mention the theory of international movements of metal, especially promoted by Ricardo. Within this basic conception which developed logically into a cost of production theory of money value, the element of supply and demand played at first only a small part. Later,

however, the quantity theory of money resulted and a new idea was produced: if the value of the monetary unit depends merely on the amount of money in existence, while the quantity of the transactions and the velocity remain constant, the idea of the value of the monetary material is bound to recede and we approach at once modern views. Thus the quantity theory represented a considerable advance; it became dominant in English literature with John Stuart Mill but did not prove very successful elsewhere. Already at an earlier period it had played an important part in practical discussions, though in the form of the 'currency theory' which is not essential to it. It was always under attack and although some positive achievements resulted from these attacks (Tooke, Fullarton), it was not overcome during this period.[1]

The classical economists were at first inclined to see an advantage for all concerned in the improvement of the methods of production, apart perhaps from the damage which might result from such an improvement for the landlord. Under the influence of contemporary discussion, however, Ricardo soon changed his mind—to the consternation of McCulloch—by trying to prove that the introduction of machines can, and in some cases must, be harmful to the interests of the worker. This proof is contained in a chapter of the *Principles* which stands entirely outside the remaining context of the book and which forms its latest part. The arguments contained in it were improved formulations of a widespread popular conception which saw in the machines the enemy of the workers—at least within the capitalist form of economy. We meet it in practically all writings on economic policy of an anti-capitalist tendency. Although Marx made most of it, his pronouncements on this theme, which contain a great many catchwords (industrial reserve army, immiseration (*Verelendung*)[2]) belong to the weakest parts of his work. These pronouncements amount substantially

[1] Of importance is also the idea, stressed by Say and J. Mill in particular, that in the long run all products are paid for only by other products. It is the basis for the idea of substituting labour-certificates for money. (Proudhon, Owen.)

[2] Translator's footnote: There is no exact English equivalent for *Verelendung*. J. A. S. himself suggests 'immiseration' in his book *Capitalism, Socialism and Democracy*.

to an argument against a different conviction, which is based on the advantages that accrue to the workers from the introduction of the machines—the theory of compensation. This theory, the most important representatives of which are Senior, McCulloch and some French economists, does not go very deeply into the matter either, and in many cases simply takes over arguments which had been derived from the popular discussion. We can do no more than refer the reader to the history of economic doctrines by Ergang and in addition perhaps to the books by Nicholson, *On Machinery*, by Mannstädt, *Kapitalistische Anwendung der Maschinerie* and to the literature quoted in this work.

It was during this period that the phenomenon of crisis moved into the scientific horizon for the first time, and with it there appeared certain explanations which practical businessmen had devised for it. The most important achievement in this field was the proof (Say, J. Mill) that a simple theory of over-production was untenable and the clarification of the simple fact, which yet was so often misunderstood, that there can be no supply without a simultaneous demand. This proof represented a great advance, even if it was overrated in its importance and was not provided with the necessary qualifications. Out of this a positive theory of crisis developed directly: Say's theory of the outlets of trade, *débouchés*, which was widely accepted, especially also by Ricardo. This theory maintained that there can be no general over-production and a fundamental disturbance of the economic equilibrium never results from production, therefore, the cause of a crisis can only be found in incorrect conditions of production, in a proportional over-production of one commodity. The most important case which can reveal such over-production is a sudden change in the channels of trade. This theory was attacked especially by Malthus—also by others such as Sismondi and Bernhardi, whose opposition, however, counted for little—from the point of view of a different conception of the economic equilibrium. This conception led to the proposition, which appears very strange to us today but was very common at the time, that the consumption of unproductive, especially of luxury goods, was necessary. This was one of the most important controversies of the period.

In addition we might mention the theory of under-consumption which was propounded by Marx with special emphasis. This theory explains crises by a discrepancy between the productive capacity and the purchasing power of society. This discrepancy results from the fact that the workers in consequence of their 'immiseration' were less and less able to take over that part of the social product that had been produced for the satisfaction of their demand. For the rest we refer the reader to the history of economic doctrines by Bergmann, to the survey by Herkner (in *Handwörterbuch der Staatswissenschaften*) and to the writings by A. Spiethoff.

Thus many other themes could be dealt with, but it must be sufficient here to sketch the general basic features of the attitude of the most important groups of economists and to give some examples of their application.

IV

THE HISTORICAL SCHOOL AND THE THEORY OF MARGINAL UTILITY

1. The more we approach modern times the less possible it becomes to characterize briefly the wealth of currents and cross-currents and the more untrue, forced and misleading appears any systematic arrangement and grouping. The slogans used to designate certain outstanding groups are much simpler than is warranted by the actual conditions. These slogans, moveover, are partly coloured by non-scientific factors—in which case we find widely different scientific efforts thrown together—and finally they appear with a claim to universal validity, while in fact in every branch of the social sciences, and often even with different problems in the same branch, conditions are different. We must add that hand in hand with the progressing specialization resulting from the increase of the subject-matter and from the advances in analysis, which turned many of the best workers into laymen in all branches except their own special ones, a tendency established itself in most recent times to break down the barriers between the various specialized branches. This tendency, in conjunction with the requirements of the educational organization, brought individuals of the most varied character, knowledge and training into contact with the same great problems. While this happened it was natural that the result was not at once a calm and fruitful exchange but at first a hopeless struggle for supremacy amongst the basic assumptions contributed by the individuals concerned. It will be even less possible for us than has been the case so far to enumerate individual achievements, if this survey is not to develop into a bibliography. We prefer to single out the two important points which have been indicated in the title of this chapter and to characterize them briefly.

2. Before we do so we must touch upon a factor which is almost

always associated with modern efforts in the field of social science but which can be kept separate as far as subject-matter is concerned—the deep, even passionate interest in *Sozialpolitik* which was felt, particularly in Germany, by the experts in our discipline.[1] The importance of this factor in itself and the political achievements of this intellectual school do not belong to a history of our science. Yet this movement powerfully affected scientific work in our field and we must at least mention this influence briefly. First, the interest in questions of *Sozialpolitik* stimulated scientific investigation of a special kind, it led people to collect and to discuss material for these questions.

If today we are relatively well informed about industrial organization, the living conditions of the working class, the effectiveness of social administration and similar questions, we owe this to this school and in particular to its centre in Germany, the *Verein für Sozialpolitik*. Secondly, this school influenced the scientific attitude of the larger public in many ways by recommending to them certain conclusions or by making them dislike others, according to whether individual theories were associated with endeavours in the field of *Sozialpolitik* or were opposed to them. Theories which employed 'social' conceptions and did not talk of individuals at all, or only little, belong to the former category; theories in which 'individualist' conceptions play an important part belong to the latter. Thirdly, preoccupation with practical questions pushed into the background that kind of penetrating analysis which never carries with it immediately practical solutions of the problems concerned, but is so important for the progress of knowledge and does not thrive in the high temperature of political interests. He who is filled with political ideals can often with the best will in the world show no enthusiasm for impractical and often Utopian investigations. He does not reach the heart of the matter if he can only achieve this by throwing himself with his whole personality into the task. From this political standpoint it is not always possible to do justice even to the work of the historian.

Without theoretical or historical tools, however, scientific work on immediately practical problems of the day resembles the day-to-

[1] Translator's footnote: The term *Sozialpolitik* is really untranslatable.

day production in the search for food. In these circumstances it becomes increasingly difficult to carry out purely scientific discussions. In opposition to this trend there developed in the period under review in Germany a reaction which manifests itself in particular in the controversy whether scientific value judgments about social events and practical proposals are admissible or even possible. Most economists have taken part in this discussion. In other countries the question was neither formulated so precisely nor discussed so vigorously. As we know it already occupied the mind of the classical economists.

3. There is another school which is in fact in most cases united with the school mentioned above but can be separated from it in principle and which is of much greater scientific importance: the 'historical school'. Its essence does not lie merely in the use it makes of historical material, since this is not peculiar to any one school exclusively and does not necessarily involve a definite point of view in scientific or practical questions. A criterion, however, which would force us to count by far the greater number of all economists of all countries and periods as members of a group which in actual fact was more limited and more clearly defined, is obviously useless for the purposes of a history of methods and doctrines.[1]

Nor does the essence of the historical school lie in those great basic conceptions which are usually described as its characteristic features and which we find without exception outside its circle as well, but in the fact that it put historical and altogether descriptive work on details into the forefront as the most important, or at any rate as the primary task, of social science. Although it is true that economists did not simply fit in with the traditional educational organization of the sciences in other respects either, and did not simply leave all historical investigation to the professional historians, it was the historical school which was the first to undertake

[1] If we wanted to count all those as members of the historical school who show an understanding for the necessity of historical material and who approve of historical studies we should not be able to enumerate half a dozen of the greater names as standing outside the historical school. Even the criterion of an occasional excursion into historical studies would, e.g. place a writer like J. Mill amongst the members of the historical school.

systematic historical work on principle. It tried to make the historical spirit, which can only be understood in connection with such systematic work, predominant in the field of the social sciences. This is the spirit which breathes in detailed historical research and it is not merely a general consciousness of the flow of events as Roscher describes it. It implied that love for a preoccupation with the material as such, that desire for an intimate understanding of the concrete and individual phenomena which accepts no formulation as final. The reason for this is that any such formulation, let alone any generalization, must appear at best as a miserable half-truth and in most cases even as a caricature in relation to the wealth of the facts which have been observed and experienced. It implies also that understanding, the highest and most subtle attraction of which cannot be described to the non-historian, but unfolds itself only to him who himself has done historical work. Nobody who does not live and has his being in historical work can understand this, any more than anybody can understand theory unless he is wrapped up in theoretical work.[1] People of different mentality turned to the two methods, and their daily work on the historical material or in the field of theory continued to shape their basic attitudes, which had been opposed to each other in any case, until in many cases it was perhaps possible for one side to comprehend logically the 'opposite school' but no longer to participate in it emotionally. In this case it became inevitable that some of the writers overrated their own approach. This, however, is a good thing, because we do not think that we are in danger of appearing too paradoxical, if we maintain that science would never have come into being unless each scholar

[1] We express one point of view precisely, although of course we do not meet it with equal precision in all followers of the historical school. Many economists who count themselves as belonging to it, particularly as the consequence of the personal relation between teacher and pupil have nothing of this specifically historical spirit. It is interesting to observe how the professional historians reacted to this school, which, as it were, was an advanced post of history. Some historians began to consider themselves as sociologists (Breysig, Lamprecht), but the majority did not altogether react in a friendly way. They held on to technical imperfections in the work of the historical economists and looked at suggestions made by them often with the narrow-mindedness of the specialist.

overrates his particular method, his own problems and what he can do for their solution. This, however, leads to a 'controversy about methods'.

It is well known that the historical school originated in Germany and experienced its golden age there. To regard as its most characteristic point the cultivation of detailed historical research which is the basis for all further work is the same thing as to say that it is associated with the name of G. von Schmoller. From the point of view of justice in the field of the history of method there are the following reasons in favour of this statement. First, a 'school', which became a force in our science and which could call forth or influence analogous movements in other countries developed only under Schmoller's leadership. We do not deprecate the work of Roscher, Hildebrand and Knies[1] if we state that they could not have brought this about. Secondly, the basic thought of the historical school is one of those cases in which what matters is not the mere demand for an historical approach but its realization. Thus Schmoller's school would still be the 'historical school' *par excellence*, even if it had merely carried out what others have described as necessary. Thirdly, however, it is quite wrong to assume that it merely elaborated as the 'younger' historical school the ideas of the 'older' school which in Germany comprised chiefly the three authors mentioned above. On the contrary, the 'historical point of view' of which Roscher and Knies talk is something quite different from that of Schmoller and his pupils. The former above all involves ideas in the field of the philosophy of history which are lacking in the latter, as, e.g., the idea of Vico and Comte of the parallel development of the various nations and the idea of the nation as an organism which can age and die.

These and similar ideas point to non-historical sources, and the

[1] Of the works of these authors the following are of greatest importance to us: Roscher, *Grundriss zu Vorlesungen über die Staatswissenschaft nach geschichtlicher Methode*, 1843; Hildebrand, *Nationalökonomie der Gegenwart und Zukunft*, 1848 (fragment) and several articles in his *Jahrbücher*. Knies *Die politische Oekonomie vom Standpunkt der geschichtlichen Methode*, 1853, second greatly enlarged edition under a somewhat different title, 1881–3. His great work *Geld und Kredit* stands quite outside the specifically historical range of ideas.

point of view of the members of the younger historical school can be characterized by their desire to eliminate these non-historical conceptions in the interests of unbiased and detailed historical study. This is true in exactly the same sense, though in a milder form, in which they wanted to eliminate the propositions of the classical 'economic sociologists'. Such an attempt is justified if it is undertaken in the name of scientific exactness and we shall have to give credit to it even if we believe that those older conceptions contained elements which were capable of further development. If, however, we leave these ideas out of Roscher's intellectual equipment we find that what remains is a theorist who happens to lay special emphasis on historical examples and who insists just as much as J. S. Mill did on the qualifications that must be made when theoretical propositions are applied in practice.[1] With Knies the matter is somewhat different. His resistance to the splitting up of the personality into individual 'urges' and to their treatment in isolation—although we must stress the fact that this does not constitute the essence of classical economic thought, as Knies thought—and the emphasis which he places on the vital part played by non-economic elements even in the field of economics (*Heteronomy of Economics*) places him more closely to the genuine historical school. Nevertheless the author of *Geld und Kredit* can be described merely as a theorist who was closely associated with history and its philosophy. If he had founded a school, which in spite of the deep effect of his text book was not the case, it would have become a school of a predominantly analytical character. With this of course we do not want to deny the existence of an intellectual relationship. We merely reject that tendency in the history of the sciences which attributes to every similarly sounding idea—particularly if the same terms are used like the term 'historical' in this case—and to every axiomatic statement, which has been detached from the essential parts of the work of an author, an importance which produces the result that the introductions to the works in

[1] He was inclined towards theoretical speculations where they were more doubtful than within the field of pure economics—in this respect the subtitle of his book on Politics: *Naturlehre der Monarchie, etc.*, and even more its contents are significant.

our discipline are of greater importance than the works themselves.

Hildebrand can be described most easily as a forerunner of the historical school. Yet he was no more than a forerunner, because this vigorous mind, who 'always criticizing' made so many stimulating suggestions and did some genuinely historical work as well while anticipating quite a few of the arguments of the historical school, remained nevertheless outside its circle. In fact he was still under the influence of the idea of the 'Law of historical development' and did not take the decisive step. He must, however, also be mentioned as a forerunner of the *Sozialpolitik* school and—though with less justification—of the marginal utility theory. Yet it would be misleading to include him simply in one of these groups because this acute critic was not positive enough in his statements to justify such an inclusion.

Next to the circle of Schmoller there stand some other personalities, such as K. Bücher, G. Knapp, L. Brentano and Inama-Sternegg, whose particular point of view cannot be discussed here in detail. If, however, we want to determine who belongs to the historical school in modern times we find that the personal point of view which we assume is just as decisive as it was in determining who belonged to it in the past. Only a few people are quite unaffected by its influence. If the question therefore is to ascertain how far its influence reached, by far the greater majority of the German economists and very many who were not Germans must be counted as members of the historical school. Those, however, who represent the type of the school in its purest form and are the genuine guardians of its spirit form only a small minority, as is the case with most schools. To these we must add groups of economists who do not work historically at all, or only occasionally, and merely agree with the broad principles of the school. This fact does not turn anybody into an economic historian any more than a scholar becomes a theorist if he acknowledges theory in general and carries out theoretical work occasionally.

If we counted all 'empiricists' as members of the historical school the latter would comprise absolutely all economists. The border-line with history proper is just as fluid. What is decisive here is the question whether economic or sociological points of view emerge more or less clearly and whether there is a tendency to comprise finally all detailed conclusions into some total conception. This, however, does not provide us with a criterion which would enable us to draw a definite line of demarcation.

4. If we inquire into the causes of the genesis and rise of the historical school we must once more recall to mind the fact that science in all periods and in all countries contained historical and theoretical elements and that both play a part in works which aim at describing the whole field and do not confine themselves merely to special questions. According to inclination and training some people turn to theoretical problems, while others apply themselves to historical and altogether descriptive ones—more exactly to problems the treatment of which involves description either as preparatory or as main work—without this in itself constituting a contradiction in principle. Nobody could have treated the problems in which Ricardo was interested in any other way than theoretically, just as nobody could have dealt with the problem of towns without having collected facts previously. With the inevitability which is so well known to anybody who knows the history of our science one or the other of the two methods of approach predominated first in the various countries and second in the same country at different times. This occurred within the limits set by the conditions in the various countries, which remained relatively constant. What demands an explanation in this context is the fact that the historical school predominated so strongly in Germany while at the same time theory was thrown overboard and that many economists regarded the collection of facts as an end in itself—at least immediately—and as their main scientific 'purpose in life' (Schmoller, article 'Volkswirtschaftslehre' in *Handwörterbuch der Staatswissenschaft*, p. 47).

Amongst the circumstances which favoured this school in general and in Germany in particular pride of place belongs to the extension of the range of interests and problems in the field of economics. The science of sociology began to make its appearance and burning problems of the day together with urgent influences from without such as the evolutionary theory made themselves felt. To a new generation wide and magnificent vistas which took them far beyond mere economics were opened up. Even within the group of economic problems people had before their eyes tasks of a magnitude not dreamt of before, while in the field of theory problems outside the sphere of pure economics were particularly attractive. Schmoller expressed for us the feeling that dominated many in his position by his exclamation: 'O century, it is a joy to live within thy bounds!'

The Universities and the official teachers of economics could not keep aloof from all this without becoming unfaithful to the important part which they played in Germany and without losing all touch with the most active forces of the time. The 'official profession', however, knew no other social science except economics —is it therefore surprising that the latter began to transform itself quickly and to extend itself *ad infinitum*?

That the scientific investigation of this wide field should have proceeded along historical lines followed, at least partly from the nature of things. For outside a small group of problems—Schmoller strikingly talks of the latter as of *one* room in a large house—the historical approach is sometimes the only possible one and is always one amongst several possible ones. What, however, remains unexplained is the fact that this historical approach was employed so exclusively and that any other approach was despised almost as amateurish and unscientific and was excluded almost completely from official economics. The explanation for this is to be found in the extremely flourishing state of historical research in Germany which established for history a dominant role in Germany's intellectual life. The Göttinger school of historians of civilization and a number of great historians starting with Niebuhr continued a tradition which had exerted a great influence before Herder and then through him. This tradition later became the basis for a general intellectual trend in the period of the romantic movement, although the range of ideas of this movement cannot be automatically described as specifically 'historical'.[1] Historio-

[1] On the other hand, the connection with Hegel, of which Schmoller talks, is not really compatible with the principle of the empirical and exact investigation of the facts, which was stressed so often by the representatives of the

graphy had reached a high level, not only taken absolutely, but its relative importance in Germany's intellectual life was even greater in comparison with the other elements in the sphere of social sciences. Amongst the latter there was nothing that was equal to it. The best minds, the most vigorous personalities in the teaching profession had devoted themselves to it. Nobody else could offer so much to all those who were attracted by the social sciences; and especially those who demanded serious work in the field of the social sciences seized above all upon history—indeed they could not seize upon anything else.

In fact, about the middle of the nineteenth century the non-historical science of economics in Germany offered very little and this was a further reason for the success of the historical school. Even if theoretical speculation could have offered everything which it is able to offer, it still would have appeared insufficient in view of the extended range of interests. A discipline which is old established and well entrenched can stand the emergence of new problems outside its range and can endure the assault of new problems of a 'topical' character which divert the general interest from it, while a discipline which is still in its initial stage will be thrown aside. The more serious and exact it is the more it is bound to be misunderstood and to be exposed to the charge that it offers stones instead of bread. Yet matters were not even like that. Theoretical economics had never become firmly entrenched in Germany, nor had it entered deeply into the consciousness of most people; it was an alien plant which, moreover, had been transplanted by hands

historical school. The philosophical element in the equipment of the German mind is, however, powerful enough to influence almost all its manifestations. Furthermore, many historical economists undoubtedly have an inclination towards philosophic speculation as such. Yet the concrete investigations of Schmoller in particular seem to us to be free from Hegelian influences, especially in contrast to the 'older' historical school in Germany. Moreover, as regards method there is a world of difference between Hegel and Schmoller's school. Nevertheless it would hardly be correct to see in the historical school a 'reaction of empiricism' against philosophy and the theoretical sciences, for, firstly, theoretical and philosophic interests do not coincide and, secondly, the only real phenomenon of the intellectual history of the nineteenth century, which can be described by the expression just mentioned, is a philosophic tendency of a positivist character with which the historian has nothing to do.

which were by no means especially skilful. Its representatives could not prove attractive and its doctrines could not possibly provide intellectual satisfaction. Thus people turned away from it and towards the new men whose minds had been formed by history. In the historical circle hardly any attempts were made to penetrate into it or to reform it but it was laid aside and condemned to death in general terms. For the next generation a thorough theoretical training was no longer a necessary precondition for taking part in the work of our discipline and theoretical works received hardly any attention any more, while the judgments on theory once they had been accepted remained the more firmly established.

Matters were different outside Germany. Not only did theory resist with more success there, but above all history never had such a dominating position there, and inasmuch as people demanded more than pure economics they employed theoretical weapons even outside its sphere. Nevertheless, even outside Germany a reaction set in and, partly independently, partly in connection with the German school, an historical school made itself felt, although the whole movement had few repercussions and did not produce such great performances nor did it become so exclusive as was the case in Germany.

In England there were, as has already been mentioned, counter currents even at the time when the classical economists flourished. A real attempt to replace the theoretical treatment of economic problems by detailed historical research was made in the *Essay on the Distribution of Wealth* by R. Jones which was not without influence and of which only the first part on the ground-rent appeared. It reveals a specifically historical opposition to theory. In the sixth decade of the century economic history which until then had only rarely been cultivated by economists for its own sake—the best achievement in this field was the book by Tooke and Newmarch, *History of Prices*, 1838–1857—became more prominent. Th. Rogers, *History of Agriculture and Prices in England*, 1866–88, started the process, he was followed by W. Cunningham, *Growth of English Industry and Commerce*, 1882, 2nd ed. 1892, and by other historians of agriculture and the law. (Seebohm, Maitland and others.) A. Toynbee, *Industrial Revolution of the Eighteenth*

Century, lectures, published in 1884, influenced wide circles and attacked energetically an unrealistic theory.

The real disciples of the German historical school, however, were Cliffe Leslie, J. K. Ingram and, later, W. J. Ashley. The two former writers, especially Leslie, opened the attack against the theoretical approach (Leslie's essay in the *Fortnightly Review*, 1879, is especially important, since it is the only orthodox presentation of the attitude of the German historical school in English).[1] Without working historically themselves these scholars present the historical arguments to the wider public. Yet although they were listened to with a certain amount of approval the negative part of their statements remained without lasting influence, because in the first place these arguments did not have behind them the positive achievements of the Germans and the German love of history and, secondly, they were opposed by much sharper criticism. What produced a storm in Germany caused merely some ripples here. Ashley's attitude already was a much more moderate one and, in so far as there developed an opposition to theory at all amongst professional economists, this opposition soon faded away. Yet the positive side of the doctrine of this English historical school bore fruit. Detailed research into historical and otherwise descriptive material prospered (S. and B. Webb, Booth and others) and economic history assumed a definite place in the academic curriculum as well; not, it is true, in the place of theoretical economics but beside it, more in the position of an auxiliary science which was also represented by special teachers.[2]

In France people—regardless of Comte—clung until modern times to the school which has been described earlier on, but this school allowed detailed historical and descriptive research to develop freely. Nowhere else can we see so clearly that there exists no

[1] Ingram, *The Present Position and Prospects of Political Economy*, 1878, is influenced by Comte. Now it is true that Comte is usually considered in historical circles as a 'precursor', but again as in the case of Hegel—only in a different direction—this belief was based on an error. What has Comte's intellectual world in common with the historical school, unless the latter is deprived of all its characteristic features?

[2] The range of ideas of Th. Buckle is outside our scope. His book, moreover, had no influence on economics.

implicit contradiction between theory and economic history and how little unbiased people doubted that both methods are equally necessary. A number of economic historians, amongst whom Levasseur and d'Avenel are outstanding, belong to the dominant school referred to above.[1] The majority of them in fact carried out research into the material of contemporary facts. In this respect Leroy-Beaulieu may be quoted as an example of a thinker who treated even economic theory from the point of view of someone who sums up individual observations of contemporary events. A. Liesse expresses the attitude of this group best by his combination of historical material and the 'Laws of human nature', of general doctrine and an interpretation of the latter which was adapted to the circumstances. Nevertheless, even here a reaction set in against this school in connection with the German historical school. The spokesmen of this reaction were primarily those professors who had been given the chairs of the faculties of Law which had been newly founded in 1878 and of whom some approached their new subject with an impartiality that had not been clouded by any previous work in their field. Cauwès is a particularly outstanding member of this circle who approached economic theory in a way similar to that of Leslie for example. Yet this movement produced few positive results and soon faded out. Ch. Guide may be mentioned as a representative of those French economists who were to some extent influenced by it and saw in it a means with which to divert French economics from its far too rigid course. Gide combined in an equal manner social-political, historical and new theoretical ideas.

We must, however, mention in addition two schools which were more indigenous. Economics in France kept more within its boundaries than it did in Germany, and French economists insisted on a clear line of demarcation between economics and the field of sociology; in consequence an independent sociology developed much more quickly than in Germany. Part of the latter of course coincides with 'economic' investigations in Germany and

[1] Compare, incidentally, a methodological study by Levasseur, *De la methode dans la science économique*, 1898, also the work of the historian Seignobos, *La methode historique appliquée aux sciences sociales*, 1901.

thus its method is of importance also for us. It would lead us too far to characterize the various groups and leading personalities, but it must be emphasized that several of these groups came very near the historical school in their method. Here belongs, e.g., Ch. Letourneau and the circle of pupils of Worms and Dürkheim. Although they did not carry out original research into archives or other primary sources, at least not for its own sake, all their investigations are based on historical, ethnological and statistical material. It was, however, not the material itself that appealed directly to the reader, but it provided the basis for generalizations. This did not constitute a difference from the historical school in principle, but in fact the difference was very great. Specialized historical research becomes less important and the border lines, as regards locality and subject matter, to which original historical research is tied, disappear. Moreover, the investigation of individual social institutions and phenomena (property, marriage, classes, etc.) becomes the immediate and only purpose. Even the historical school, it is true, sometimes worked in the same way, but so far had done so only occasionally, as a side line. This school likewise produced a great many methodological works. (Above all Dürkheim, *Règles de la methode sociologique*, 1895; Clément, *Essai sur la science sociale*, 1867; Fouillée, *Le mouvement positiviste et la conception sociologique*, and more recently the work by Simiand which expresses the point of view of these groups and their dislike of theory, which is common to them all, most clearly.)

Secondly, we have to consider the school of Leplay. Leplay's chief works are: *Les ouvriers Européens*, 1st ed. 1855, 2nd ed. 1844–1879; *La reforme sociale*, 1st ed. 1864; *L'Organisation du travail*, 1870; *L'organisation de la famille*, 1872; *Constitution essentielle de l'humanité*, 1880; he also founded the series of monographs *Les ouvriers des deux mondes* and the periodicals *La reforme sociale*. We might further mention as successors Du Maroussem, Cheysson and C. Jannet, who often had an independent approach. Their ideas on *Sozialpolitik*, which were the main concern for Leplay, do not interest us in this context. The more important, however, is his method of a detailed investigation of the living conditions of the working class by taking the individual worker's family and especially its budget into consideration. It is evident that this method, which since then has been employed also in Germany, America and England is not only absolutely necessary for some specialized problems, but can also make a valuable contribution to our general understanding of social developments. That so far it had not led to any results which could be formulated briefly is inherent in its nature and does not imply an objection. The more general statements of Leplay, however, are scientifically not very valuable, partly because they did not suit his talent, partly because he completely lacked any, even the most elementary, economic training. This robs his attacks against the classical economists in particular of any significance and it is quite clear that he can hardly have read them.[1]

In America, Italy, Holland and northern Europe a genuine historical movement did not develop. Even there, however, we find an increase in 'descriptive economics'. In America, moreover, scholars began to co-operate on a large scale in the work of description, operating according to a plan (within the Carnegie Institute, the Smithsonian Institution and, furthermore, in the Documentary History of American Industrial Society). Yet this increase was equalled by the growth of theoretical speculation and went hand in hand with it. That specifically historical spirit which alone turns the collection of facts, which after all is necessary for any school, into something methodologically distinct, did not develop. Occasionally the critical points of view of the historical school evoked an echo, but only a weak one, particularly outside the circle of the leading economists, and they had little positive effect. It is difficult to answer with a clear conscience the question which is of such interest to the member of the historical or the theoretical party in Germany, which of the schools 'predominates'. Judging by the number of volumes the 'investigation of facts' predominates of course, as is everywhere the case. According to the criterion, however, of where the achievements of economists of reputation could

[1] The lovable but not very powerful personality of E. de Laveleye (main work *Ureigentum*) also deserves to be mentioned: a man full of high ideals in the field of *Sozialpolitik* and of predominantly historical inclinations, he was one of the best representatives of a type fairly frequently found during this period.

be found, it was the theory that predominated. It is possible to obtain a general view which is not too unreliable by comparing, say, the contents of the publications of the American Economic Association, the position of which in America has at least some resemblance to that of the *Verein für Sozialpolitik* in Germany, with the contents of the publications of the latter, or by studying the American and Italian text-books. We must do so, however, by considering their subject-matter and not merely their axiomatic statements.

5. This survey has shown how little a methodological controversy about principles was inherent in the subject-matter. If this is so, however, what then were the causes of this controversy? What was it all about? And was the whole struggle really necessary, which wasted so much strength that might have produced positive work instead, and which separated men who were so worthy of mutual esteem and who might have offered so much if they had calmly collaborated? To philosophize about this question and to state with sentimental regrets how nice it would have been if things had turned out differently would be the same as to fall into an antiquated kind of historiography. We have, however, already suggested an explanation for the controversy: it was a struggle between two methods of work, between people of different mental habits, who fought for elbow room or for domination. This explains, moreover, the way in which the controversy was conducted and its results: as in a political struggle it was in the first place the battle-cry which touched many sensitive minds and awoke certain ideas and emotions much more than did elaborate arguments. Furthermore each argument produced its effect by itself, that is, independently of accompanying or contrasting arguments, without being co-ordinated in a person's consciousness with the other arguments or without being considered carefully in comparison with the counter-arguments. Hence the endless repetition of arguments which had already been refuted as thoroughly as could have been desired.

In everything which the parties have to say to each other there is always a reminder of the invincible dislike for either the theoretical 'phantom' or the historical 'drudgery'. This dislike is not amenable to any merely logical argument. Again and again we find the tendency of the parties to reproach each other with being unscientific and to adorn themselves with epithets which they consider as denoting their own excellence (realistic, exact, modern, etc.). We find this tendency often next to the admission that there is something justifiable in the opponents' point of view. The individual arguments themselves—and even more the way in which they were emphasized and formulated—changed on both sides, sometimes very abruptly. This makes it almost impossible to ascribe to an author a definite statement without confronting it with other contradictory and opposing statements. For this reason and also because it is difficult today to ascertain the precise meaning of individual utterances we shall content ourselves with a few remarks. After all it would hardly be fair to take seriously every statement which had been made in the heat of the battle.

In its early stages the historical school directed its attack in the first place with almost complete success against the political and social philosophical theses of the old school of economists, against Manchester Liberalism, individualism, rationalism, etc. In doing so its representatives also rejected theory as such and described it as scholastic, speculative, naturalistic, etc. There was, moreover, a tendency to doubt whether the conception of laws could be applied to social science at all, but this was not of primary importance. If Schmoller, e.g. described any follower of Smith as unfit to teach economics he obviously had in mind the social-philosophical and political elements in Smith's doctrine. From this phase we must distinguish another, not so much chronologically but as regards subject-matter, in which a more detailed discussion of the problem of methods takes place. In this the advantages of induction and deduction, the justification for, or, as the case may be, the possibility of isolating problems were discussed. This phase was not very fruitful. What was at the root of the controversy about induction and deduction was by no means a logical problem but simply the difference between the collection of facts and their analysis. Nevertheless, for some time the struggle was waged in this guise which did not suit it at all and, needless to say, did not produce any notable results. Slogans like 'economics in the void',

'Atomism', etc. also belong here. A third phase was under the influence of advances in epistemology and of the discussions on method which were conducted by professional historians. This phase produced a new complication since now epistemological differences, which in themselves have nothing to do with economic method, were dragged into the discussion; nevertheless it brought about without a doubt a clarification of views.

In the centre of the discussion there stands the great methodological achievement of C. Menger: *Untersuchungen über die Methode der Sozialwissenschaften und der politischen Oekonomie insbesondere.* It led people out of the stage of observation and individual arguments and attempted to clarify the struggle about methods by a thorough discussion of principles. In doing so it defended the theoretical position against the misunderstandings to which it had been exposed.[1] In this respect there was indeed a great deal to be done. With the specifically historical range of ideas there was closely connected the view that economic theory was not in any way based on the observation of facts but on premises of a dubious character, that it was fundamentally prescientific and was destined to be replaced by a serious investigation of the facts. In consequence it was assumed that the task of science in the field of economic theory was not to develop it further but merely to describe it and to explain its ever-changing systems in historical terms. At

[1] The following writers have the same basic approach: Böhm-Bawerk, 'Method in Political Economy', *Annals of American Academy*, 1; v. Philippovich, *Ueber Aufgabe und Methode der Politischen Oekonomie*, 1886; Sax, *Wesen und Aufgaben der Nationalökonomie*, 1884; Dietzel, 'Beiträge zur Methodik der Wirtschaftswissenschaften', *Conrad's Jahrb.* 1884, and other works; Lifschitz, *Untersuchungen über die Methodologie der Wirtschaftswissenschaft*, 1909. Also the following English writers on methodology: Jevons, 'The Future of Political Economy', *Fortnightly Review*, 1876, and 'Principles of Science', 1874; Cairnes, *The Character and Logical Method of Political Economy*, 1875; Keynes, *Scope and Method of Political Economy*, 1st ed 1891, and article 'Method' in Palgrave's Dictionary. Bagehot's attitude (*Economic Studies*, ed. 1880) is similar to that of K. Bücher: With these two thinkers theory appears indispensable for an understanding of the events in the modern exchange economy, beyond this, however, it is without any value. Furthermore, we find methodological discussions of a similar character in most of the systematic works, e.g. in A. Wagner, Philippovich, G. Cohn, J. Conrad, Seligman, Marshall and others.

best it might be possible to recognize the establishment and elaboration of a system of conceptions which could be put at the disposal of a science of society as a task of a theoretical nature, though of comparatively secondary importance.

It was also believed that it was hardly possible any longer to talk of 'laws' in the field of social science and that at best it might be possible to talk of such regularities as can be discovered by detailed historical and statistical research. These 'regularities' might possibly be termed 'empirical laws'. The term 'theory' became so outlawed that it is today sometimes replaced by that of 'intellectual reproduction' or 'doctrine', in order not to evoke from the start a whole host of prejudices. And even if 'theory' in the sense of generally valid concepts was not regarded as absolutely impossible, the existing theory was considered as wrong in principle. Although Menger opposed these views he recognized at once the necessity of an historical basis for the solution of a great many economic problems and he considered such an historical basis essential for the investigation of individual cases. Schmoller[1] retorted in a polemical form which was necessitated by the occasion, but as regards the subject-matter his approach was by no means simply a negative one. Already at this time he recognized not only that some of Menger's critical observations were justified but also how essentially similar the causal nexus in social science and natural science is; he also described the explanation of social phenomena in the form of cause and effect and in the form of laws—for him at this time both coincided—as the aim of scientific effort. Indeed we find even the far-reaching proposition that all perfect science is 'deductive', that is, that the state of ideal perfection is only reached when it has become possible to explain concrete phenomena completely with the help of theoretical premises.

This proposition implies the acknowledgment that such a state of the science is possible in principle—even if in actual fact it

[1] *Zur Methodologie der Staats-und Sozialwissenschsften*, Jahrbuch für Gesetzgebung, 1883; comp. also *Zur Literaturgeschichte der Staats und Sozialwissenschaft*, 1888, and *Wechselnde Theorien und feststehende Wahrheiten* . . ., 1897; earlier statements by Schmoller on questions of method can be found in the symposium *Grundfragen der Sozialpolitik und Volkswirtschaftslehre*, 1898.

should remain unattainable for us. It also implies a complete rejection of the specifically historical belief in the 'incalculable' and essentially 'irrational' nature of social events. Schmoller goes further here than most of the theorists would have been prepared to do. In his works on method in the *Handwörterbuch der Staatswissenschaften* he emphasises the causal and theoretical task of social science even more forcefully. This approach is quite compatible with his view that the theory of social science needs to a large extent an historical 'substructure'. All these statements do not at all reveal an opposition to theory on principle, although of course they do not exclude an opposition to the existing theory. This latter kind of opposition, however, could only be an opposition 'within the theory', because as soon as the historian sets out to obtain general perceptions on the basis of his detailed historical research he would be forced to isolate facts and to arrive at abstractions, that is, he would in fact change into a theorist. It does not matter what these general perceptions are called. As v. Schmoller strikingly remarks, it makes no difference whether we talk of laws or whether we employ a different term for a complex of facts which remains essentially the same whatever name we might give to it. It is true that 'empirical laws', that is the identification of regularities in facts which remain unanalysed, would be possible even without abstractions, but they would, firstly, not be numerous and would, secondly, not tell us very much, they would be 'incomprehensible'.

It is interesting to observe how closely representatives of schools, which are usually considered as essentially hostile, approached each other when they came to debate the principles of the matter. Even some of Schmoller's followers, as, e.g. Hasbach[1], assumed the attitude which is characterized by the recognition of generally valid

[1] 'Ein Beitrag zur Methodologie der Nationalökonomie', *Schmoller's Jahrbücher*, 1885, and 'Mit welcher Methode werden die Gesetze der theoretischen Oekonomie gefunden', *Conrads Jahrbücher*, 1894. Yet not all did so. Apart from methodological works of an historical point of view already mentioned we may quote: Grabski, 'Zur Erkenntnislehre der volkswirtschaftlichen Erscheinungen', *Tübinger Zeitschrift*, 1861; Held, 'Uber den gegenwärtigen Prinzipienstreit in der Nationalökonomie, *Preussische Jahrbücher*, 1872; Rümelin, 'Ueber den Begriff des sozialen Gesetzes', *Reden und Aufsätze*, I, 1875. The points of view of these authors, however, differ from each other.

laws. Gradually this attitude began to prevail until finally in recent times any *argumentative* hostility to theory died out, and the distinction which had already been stressed by Menger between the perception of the general and the individual was recognized. This distinction was given philosophical support. (Windelband: 'nomothetical' and 'ideographic' point of view, Rickert: 'scientific' and 'historical' approach.) This, however, had only very little effect on the contrast which continued to exist between the two methods of work, and it was rather because people became tired of the controversy than because they composed their differences that the quarrel gradually became less bitter.

A new generation—even of supporters of the historical school—no longer intended to continue with the mere collection of facts, while in the meantime economic theory had gained new life. There could no longer be any question of overcoming the latter. With this the methodological discussion lost its polemical point and a change of theme resulted: people set out to investigate the epistemology of history[1], they started to see sociological problems in the ideas employed by the historians. Yet we cannot deal with this movement which had such a great future in front of it. In spite of all this, there often remained traces of the old popular conception about the nature of theoretical speculation and in particular the old polemical phrases survived. Indeed the latter penetrated only in recent times into the wider public, after science had already passed beyond them, which is not surprising as the views of the 'public' are always a beat behind those of science.

While people began to agree on problems of method in their original sense, today such an agreement has been rendered more difficult by a reaction against the historical school, which springs from various sources. The historical school had associated itself with political trends in the same way in which the classical econ-

[1] cf. especially the works of Max Weber, 'Roscher und Knies und die logischen Probleme der historischen Nationalökonomie', *Schmoller's Jahrbücher*, 1903–05, 'Die Objektivität sozialwissenschaftlicher Erkenntnis', *Archiv für Sozialwissenschaft*, XIX and 'Kritische Studien auf dem Gebiet der kulturwissenschaftlichen Logik', *ibidem* XXII. It is impossible for us to deal here with the large historical and epistemological literature of recent years.

omists had done in their time. And like the latter they now had to pay the price for this. The most important scientific cause of this reaction, however, is the general tendency of our time in favour of theory. Just as the historical school of economics in its heyday was an element of a general tendency towards the science of the mind and just as then the problem was how to 'base uniformly all sciences of the mind on historical-social actualities' (Schmoller), so today the current flows in an opposite direction. And we have every prospect of seeing the unpleasant spectacle that the historical school suffers the same injustice which in its time it had inflicted on the theorists. In this respect the fate of economics is analogous to that of jurisprudence. The sharp reaction against the Law of Nature at the beginning of the nineteenth century, which is associated with the names of Savingy and Eichhorn, led to the supremacy of an historical trend to which economic historians have always pointed as a model. The existing spokesmen of the Law of Nature were more and more pushed into the background and regarded with increasing contempt until it was expected that their range of ideas would disappear completely. Significantly these ideas were more and more relegated into a 'history of the philosophy of law', in a way quite similar to the one which people employed in theoretical economics.

Yet the Law of Nature did not disappear. It survived and towards the end of the nineteenth century there appeared symptoms of a reviving movement within its confines. This movement soon gained the upper hand. This was by no means merely a revival of the 'conceptual jurisprudence' which the historical school had justifiably esteemed so little and which, though it is practically indispensable, is scientifically of very little interest. On the contrary the new movement attacked it just as energetically as the historical school had done. What the new movement did was to comprehend theoretically the phenomenon of law and the logic of law, that is to say, to move away from a specifically historical course. As far as details are concerned, the situation is quite different in the two fields. This is so already because of the difference in the nature and the function of the two. Moreover, Menger was completely right when he stated a fundamental difference between the legal and the economic historical schools. Yet the method of work and their basic features are essentially similar, nor can it be overlooked that their fate developed along parallel lines.

6. We should like to insert here a few remarks on a theme which is usually mentioned in connection with a discussion on method: the so-called mathematical method. Already in the early stages we find algebraic symbols in connection with arguments in the field of social science in the writings of some authors (Hutcheson for instance, sometimes even earlier). There is nothing extraordinary in this in principle. Whether you express general propositions in words or, for the sake of greater precision, in algebraic symbols, does not alter their essential nature at all. Moreover, whether in complicated cases one uses hypothetical numerical examples or in their place algebraic forms, is quite irrelevant in principle, it only means that the clarity and precision of the algebraic form makes all assumptions stand out more distinctly and frees the argument from the chances that are inherent in numbers which have been chosen concretely. Thus Whewell, *Cambridge Philosophical Transactions*, Vol. 3, expressed some of Ricardo's theorems in the more perfect form of algebra. This was done more often later on. How suitable this method is for a penetrating analysis can be seen in the elegant works of v. Bortkiewicz on the foundations of the Marxian system which we quoted in the preceding section.

Cournot (*loc. cit.*) founded a different kind of 'mathematical economics', which is based on the fact that the forms of thought of higher analysis can be applied very well to a number of economic propositions. These forms of higher analysis allow the investigation to be continued at such points where scientific language fails because of its clumsiness. The conception of function exists patently or latently in most purely economic arguments, and as far as the task consists in comprehending the general relations between variable quantities and in deducing from the latter as much as is possible with regard to their variation, mathematical analysis is absolutely *the* suitable instrument. Moreover, the description of economic relations in systems of simultaneous equations in itself provides a survey of the former which cannot be obtained in such a precise form in any other way. Cournot found a successor in Walras, whom we shall meet again later on and the latter was succeeded by Pareto, *Manuel*, 1908, who in essential points surpassed all his predecessors (School of Lausanne).

In England Jevons had proceeded along the same path, later Marshall and Edgeworth did so with greater success and so did J. Fisher in America. By far the most important work of this school in German is the study by R. Auspitz and R. Lieben, *Untersuchungen über die Theorie der Preise* (1888); Launhardt, *Mathematische Begründung der Volkswirtshaftslehre*, 1886, merely followed Walras and Jevons. In its early stages this school had to fight quite a few prejudices which were rooted in the dislike for employing a language incomprehensible to the larger public, and which saw in 'mathematical economics' something that was *sui generis* in principle and represented an illicit approach to the natural sciences. Gradually people began to realize that it was not essentially different from theory altogether and that it can be met only by arguments which are valid also for the latter, furthermore that it borrows nothing from natural sciences except a special technique which is quite as universally 'valid' as are the 'fundamental laws of logic'. Today this method is almost universally recognized and applied outside Germany. This applies also to France, where the resistance against it had been particularly strong. Its range of application, however, is limited and its achievements go only in some points beyond a more correct and precise presentation—this, however, means a great deal in praxi. In consequence, it is quite possible to discuss the problem whether at present it is expedient and worth while for an economist, who is primarily concerned with the acquisition of theoretical knowledge to make himself familiar with a special apparatus.[1] After all it was this question of expediency which formed the core of the basic arguments used by the opponents of the method who were indeed quite indifferent to it.

7. Let us briefly indicate some of the essential points of view which resulted from detailed historical research and which the historical school helped to establish generally.

[1] Information about the mathematical method can best be obtained from the article by Pareto in the *Enzyklopädie der mathematischen Wissenschaften* and from Edgeworth's article in Palgrave's Dictionary.

I. *The point of view of relativity.* By this is meant not the epistemological thesis that all knowledge is adapted to a special purpose inherent in one's viewpoint outside of which it has no validity, but a special kind of relativity peculiar to our field. First of all, detailed historical research teaches us better than any other method how untenable the idea is that there are generally valid practical rules in the field of economic policy. The historical school, indeed, always stressed this point of view, even within the boundaries of scientific knowledge. Although we find this view also in some of the theorists—even in Ricardo and Marx—it was never expressed with such systematic consistency. As far, however, as there was a tendency to use the argument of the 'historical causation' of social events in order to combat the possibility of generally valid knowledge—general laws—altogether, it was soon suppressed.

II. *The point of view of the unity of social life and of the inseparable correlation between its elements.* To this point of view research into historical material was bound to lead likewise, even if it could not do so unaided. The concrete facts offered by historical research cannot be dissected without loss and the historian objects to having to strip of its leaves the flower which he had picked. Hence his desire to replace the schemes of theoretical speculation by a comprehensive view of the whole of reality, a desire, the logical form of which is the argument of the heteronomy of the economy. This idea—it is indeed unfortunately a phantom—could not be maintained and Schmoller in his formulation abandons it. Yet there remained the tendency to go beyond the confines of a mere economic doctrine and a contempt for the 'experts who never follow a hare into the next field'.[1] Modern epistemology with its precise

[1] There was even a tendency to venture into regions without any bounds. The further the development of the individual discipline in the field of social science progresses, the more nebulous and remote becomes the idea of universal social science and the more imperfect any summary is bound to become. To abandon the specialized discipline of economics almost means the abandonment of the possibility of progress itself, since the economist would be alienated from his task. And yet this abandonment was almost complete in Germany. In this respect the remark in the preface to the *Schmollerfestgabe* that it is doubtful whether we can speak of a uniform economic science at all is very significant. In fact there is hardly a theme of which it would be

distinction between real and cognitive objects and the realization that in this respect matters are the same in social sciences as in the natural sciences—in nature, too, there exists an indissoluble connection between all phenomena—have greatly limited the field of controversy on this point.

III. *The anti-rationalist point of view.* People derived from history comparatively late—and completely only under the influence of extra-historical factors—one of its most distinct and valuable lessons: that of the multiplicity of motives and of the small importance of a merely logical insight where human actions are concerned. The historian who tries to understand, however possible or impossible this may be, the motives of the actors sees only rarely simple ones and almost never clear and fully conscious ones. He sees people act according to rules which have not been reasoned out and often appear to them as imperatives which cannot be discussed; or he sees people under the influence of obviously illogical impulses. It is not merely the historian who sees this, but it was the historical school above all which established this point of view in economics. At first it did so in the form of an ethical argument—hence the name 'ethical school'—and later in the form of a desire for a more complete psychology of the individual and above all the masses. For this the historical school deserves considerable credit, notwithstanding the fact that it was wrongly believed that this approach involved an objection to pure theory and that the latter would gain if its psychological foundations were to be improved. Pure theory is in the first place independent of a doctrine of motivation and is nothing less than a natural philosophy of egoism; in the second place the clearly conscious economic motive, always within the given range of vision of the participant in the economy, naturally plays such a large part in economic matters that it would indeed be worth while to deal with it in isolation if this were necessary. It is true, however, that the mere identification of ethical motives does not get us very far, but if we want to study social psychology at all, we can do so only upon new foundations and not on the old rationalist ones.

possible to extract from some economists the statement that they are not interested in it.

It is understandable that, to repeat a good expression of Graham Wallas's *Human Nature in Politics*, 1906, the exclusive consideration of a few clearly conscious motives impresses some people in the same way in which we would be impressed if an anatomist declared that he intended to disregard the existence of the liver in the human body. It is true that matters are different in economics from anatomy, but nobody takes much notice of this.

IV. *The point of view of evolution.* This point of view was indeed not unknown to theoretical speculation, compare, e.g. Marx. In fact almost all academic theoretical systems have tried to indicate the motive forces of evolution and a chapter 'on progress' was a component part of every text-book. Although this point of view could be reached also from different intellectual positions—compare, e.g. Spencer and sociology altogether—it impresses itself above all upon the historian, since he has to deal almost exclusively with changing facts. It was all the more possible to believe that within the orbit of the problem of evolution, history offered everything that could be offered, as in this approach it was much more difficult and appeared much less rewarding to isolate phenomena than if conditions were merely intellectually reconstructed. Moreover, it is certain that evolutionary theories are bound to make much greater use of historical material.

V. *The point of view of the interest in individual correlations.* It has often been expressed and still more often been instinctively assumed that in the field of social sciences we are much less concerned with the study of the general nature of events than with an investigation of concrete, individual correlations. What matters is how concrete events and conditions establish themselves and what their concrete causes are, not the general causes of social events altogether, be it that the latter are uninteresting or self-evident. In fact, the individual battle and the individual combination of facts which caused it is much more important to us than, for instance the individual combination of causes by which a tree is turned into a distinguishable individual specimen. It will always be a task of the social sciences to state such concrete causations of phenomena which interest us, and this task will always fall to social history and description, apart from its other task of providing material for the solution of a great number of general problems.

In this respect people forget, however, firstly, that this fact constitutes merely a difference in degree from natural science, for what matters within the latter as well is often the individual difference of a certain causation (the same is true of all 'applied' sciences). They forget, secondly, that the investigation of the general nature of things is in itself interesting, even if that interest is not an exclusive one, thirdly, that without such an investigation even the task of all concrete causal research cannot be performed at all, or at least not in a scientifically satisfactory manner. In spite of the credit which is due to this point of view it cannot be said that the scholars who held it made a valuable contribution to a better understanding of the nature of our discipline. Its chief merit lies in the fact that people acted in accordance with it and thus achieved great things in working for forty years on this partial task. Whether people went too far in translating this point of view into practice, as is today often maintained, everyone can judge only for himself. We do not know of a single complex of facts for which so many individual data and correlations have been brought together that we might say we had had enough of it and need not concern ourselves with it any longer. That in this process the theory suffered irreparable damage is a different matter and was, incidentally, at least to some extent inevitable.

VI. *The organic point of view.* What is always disagreeable to the historian beyond all measure is the mechanistic conception of social facts. It is true, this became a catchword in the concrete application of which people never asked themselves which of the many possible meanings of the term 'mechanistic' could be employed for a certain proposition which they opposed. The organic conception, the analogy of the social body to a physical one, was more closely associated with the historical school. Yet this school never participated in the exaggeration of this point of view, as we find it, e.g. in Schäffle, but it always stressed the fact that economics cannot be split up into an agglomeration of independent economic individuals and that economic phenomena are not merely the resultants of individual components. It showed no understanding at all for the fact that the organic conception might justifiably be employed in purely theoretical speculations in spite of all its limitations. The organic conception under the influence of Adam Müller was stated originally in the form that the national economy exists outside and above the various individual economies. To-day, however, this view has been overcome almost completely and has been replaced by a conception (compare Schmoller, article 'Volkswirtschaft', *loc. cit.*) which stresses the fact that the individual economies, which together comprise the national economy, stand in intimate mutual relations with each other. These relations are far more important than the ones which economic theory describes and which influence the individual member of the economy. They enforce in fact upon the individual a behaviour which is of a different kind and which must be explained in a way which is quite different from the one of which economic theory speaks. History in itself, however, does not produce a theory of this behaviour, this is the task of mass psychology which indeed uses historical material and was greeted sympathetically in historical circles. Moreover, since the sum total of these mutual relations comprises the 'purely economic' ones as well, this formulation of the nature of national economy merely meant that theory dealt only with part of the elements which explain social events, a fact which is always stressed by its most convinced representatives. Though this deprives this formulation of its critical point, its positive importance remains the same. The nature of the method of detailed research makes it impossible to report on its results briefly and we intend, therefore, to turn to the advances that were made in the theoretical field.

8. The revival of theoretical analysis began in the seventies and became apparent to most people in the nineties. This revival does not alter the fact that theoretical speculation, as opposed to the interest in investigations of facts, and economic theory in particular, as opposed to the wealth of problems of a different kind in the field of the social sciences, no longer played the part which it had played in the classical period. At that time economics was the only fully developed social science and gave most elegant, brief and peremptory answers to questions the difficulty of which most people underestimated. The economists who wanted to say

something about contemporary problems or about the problem of social life as such now had to enter other fields of the social sciences. He easily acquired a kind of contempt for the purely economic field, the relatively small extent of which had now become clear. This did not prevent economics from continuing to develop as a specialized discipline but it made its progress more difficult, because people found it more difficult to understand it and therefore turned to other fields. This was already apparent on the surface, but if we look more closely we find that the situation was in fact even worse: economists who described themselves as quite indifferent to theory were indeed rare, but those who had only a loose connection with it, amounting merely to a more or less critical acceptance of certain basic features, were in the majority, while those who devoted all their energy to theory were a small minority. This fact is essential for an understanding of the development of theoretical economics in this period.

The so-called theory of marginal utility was the new ferment which has changed the inner structure of modern theory into something quite different from that of the classical economists. On it depended the revival, to which we have already referred. We find traces of the ideas which this theory was to elaborate already very early on, e.g. in the writings of the scholastics (Beil) and later in those of the representatives of the Law of Nature (Pufendorf). This is quite understandable since the theory of marginal utility, like almost all scientific 'basic ideas', is extremely simple when taken by itself and without all its elaborations. We find more of it in Genovesi and Galiani, but above all in Condillac.[1] In the nineteenth century many German economists, amongst whom v. Hermann was outstanding, had proceeded half-way towards a theory of marginal utility, and it was during this period that we find in the fantastic but bold book by H. H. Gossen, *Gesetze des menschlichen Verkehrs*, 1836, the first formulation of the theory of

1 *Le commerce et le gouvernement considerés relativement l'un à l'autre*, 1776; one of the most original works of the eighteenth century. As an economist Condillac stands on the shoulders of the Physiocrats, whose doctrine he successfully supplemented just at its weakest point, the theory of value. Yet the outward success of the book was small, as was also the case with Isnard's *Traité des richesses*, 1781, which is on the same level.

marginal utility, which he stated fully conscious of its importance. It received no attention whatsoever. Dupuit (two articles in the *Annales des Ponts et Chaussées*, 1884 and 1849) and L. Walras are hardly less important. Here belongs R. Jennings, *Natural Elements of Political Economy*, 1855, in whose book we find the law of satiated demand—in the midst of a mass of phrases and proposals of little value in which the author strangely resembles Gossen—and H. D. Maccleod. In the sixth decade those works were composed which founded the system of the theory of marginal utility: Karl Menger's *Grundsätze der Volkswirtschaftslehre* appeared in 1871, W. S. Jevons, *Theory of Political Economy* was also published in 1871, after he had stated his basic ideas already in 1862 in a lecture which was published in the *Journal of the Royal Statistical Society*; Walras' *Elements d'Economie politique pure* appeared in 1874 (its decisive points had appeared already in a memoir in 1873). In the eighth decade there followed Böhm-Bawerk ('Grundzüge der Theorie des wirtschaftlichen Güterwerts', *Conrads Jahrb.* 1886; *Kapital und Kapitalzins*, Vol. 2, 1st ed. 1884 and 1888, Vol. 1, 2nd ed. 1902, Vol. 2, 3rd ed. 1912, and v. Wieser, *Ursprung und Hauptgesetze des wirtschaftlichen Wertes*, 1884; *Der natürliche Wert*, 1889.

This school in its early stages encountered roughly the following conditions amongst the circle of the theorists: in France a school predominated which derived directly from Say and was in consequence not favourably disposed towards the marginal utility theory from the beginning. Most of the authors, as for instance Block, *Progres de la science econ. depuis A. Smith*, 1891, Molinari, Y. Guyot, Leroy Beaulieu, etc., accepted its basic principle without demur, though with a certain apathy which at first prevented its further development. These authors also raised explicit objections to Walras' mathematics which they viewed with distrust. This distrust robbed Walras of any influence for a long time. We might have expected to find a similar situation in Germany, but the school, whose outstanding representatives were Hermann and Thünen, had lost its position at this time under the impact of the works of Rodbertus and Marx, which also produced a Ricardo renaissance. Very quickly an orthodox Marxian school developed under the leadership of Engels and Kautsky, and even those minds that did not belong to this school but were interested in theory turned in the first place to Rodbertus and the English classical economists, above all to Ricardo.

These writers saw in the marginal utility theory an innovation of doubtful value and started to attack its principles. In this respect they enjoyed the sympathy of their professional colleagues who did not primarily participate in theoretical speculations and were accordingly not favourably inclined towards a new theoretical structure, while they valued the old one in its historical role in spite of their doctrinal opposition. In England Jevons' attack on Ricardo and Mill had at first merely annoyed the theorists and even produced the result that the few—and little respected—remaining representatives of the classical theory rallied the more determinedly round the two names mentioned. Nevertheless the attack met with approval amongst the wider public, but almost entirely because an attack was made at all.

Only in Italy where indeed the idea of marginal utility had suggested itself already at an early period, and where it was not necessary to overcome a strong 'indigenous' school, did the economists unreservedly accept the main outlines of the new doctrine after some time. These economists soon began to elaborate the theory in a manner which was original in many respects. The Dutch did the same.

This reception itself and the further development of the doctrine can be explained by the fact that the theory of marginal utility did not originate as a widespread movement on well-prepared ground, but through the actions of some eminent men who could make their way only with difficulty and who succeeded only slowly in training a circle of disciples. They were forced to overcome singly and through the mere force of the written argument the indifference or opposition of large groups of economists who were firmly entrenched and uniformly led. The 'intellectualist error' which suggests itself so readily to us when we consider the history of a science makes us easily forget that without external help a new school can establish itself only under great difficulties, because without such help its ideas do not become known in the brief period of its formation to a sufficiently large circle of potential pupils, and the daily literary guerilla war cannot be waged because of the lack of a corresponding 'second line of defence'.[1] Especially in Germany and France, in view of the importance which is attached to academic teaching in the scientific life of these two countries, the additional factor must be taken into account that the supporters of Walras were almost completely excluded from chairs in French universities and the supporters of Menger from German ones.[2] Thus it becomes understandable that a long period during which the marginal utility theory was disregarded was followed by a period of attack. The latter was based on incomplete acquaintance with the theory and in part even on misunderstandings of it. Certain catchwords became established which appeared as final not only to the larger public, in as far as it heard of the existence of the theory of marginal utility at all, but also to the experts who were not associated with the theory. This made it almost impossible to find an unbiased circle of listeners or readers.

In this connection we must mention the charge that the theory of marginal utility was a form of 'Manchester liberalism'. The success of this attack does not alter the fact that the theory of marginal utility had nothing materially in common with the trends

[1] It is instructive for reasons of comparison to look at the way in which such revolutions were carried out elsewhere; in our field the Physiocrats are the best example. At first they merely had to conquer a very small Parisian circle, a task for which they were very favourably placed, and the general prestige of French literature helped them on as far as the outside world was concerned. A great example from a different field is the way in which the idea of evolution established itself. The strategist of the movement was Lyall. Not only did he wait until all decisive weapons had been well completed, but it was also decided by him that geology should be chosen as the first target because of its comparatively innocuous character. Then Lyall addressed personally all the leading English contemporary geologists (we do not know whether this included foreign ones as well) and convinced or 'neutralized' most of them, which was particularly easily done on English soil. And then he fired—at once with decisive success. Such strategy was alien to the three founders of the theory of marginal utility, and even if they had wanted to adopt it, they had no opportunity of doing so. In consequence their contemporaries continued quietly to cling to the traditional doctrine.

[2] The representatives of the theory of marginal utility are usually also described as belonging to the 'Austrian' school. At first, however, they formed even in Austria a small minority which encountered determined resistance.

of the Manchester school in the field of economic policy. Two of the founders of the marginal utility school propounded fairly radical views in the field of *Sozialpolitik* while the third, Walras, was a Socialist, though not an orthodox one. The struggle, once it had started, made it also more difficult to accept the theory of marginal utility, even when closer acquaintance with it had induced many people to hold a more favourable opinion. Moreover, it produced a situation in which people continued to protest formally, even though there was no longer anything that separated the combatants, and in which they stressed in an exaggerated manner secondary and unimportant points of difference. This discussion, whether the principles of the theory of marginal theory are correct, has continued to the present day. We can mention here merely the controversy between Böhm-Bawerk and Dietzel.[1]

For a considerable period, however, it has not been the theory itself but its importance and its applicability that has been in the forefront of the discussion. Moreover, it has passed its zenith and it has to an ever-increasing degree become tacitly accepted. This change occurred at first in England and it was in particular A. Marshall who, following Mill as a leader (though only in the narrow field of economics) directed English theory carefully and slowly, but the more effectively for that, on to the new course. He always showed sympathy and respect for the classical economists and regarded Jevons and the Austrians coolly and critically, while he rarely mentioned Walras at all. Yet in fact he had taken over their whole doctrine, particularly that of Walras so that it would be possible to omit those points in which he deviates from them, without an attentive reader noticing the change. We find in him merely the form, not the essence, of the classical approach and of the characteristic classical propositions. Moreover, a close contact

[1] Dietzel opened the attack with his treatise: 'Die klassische Werttheorie, und die Theorie vom Grenznutzen', *Conrads Jahrbücher*, Neue Folge, 20, to which at first Zuckerkandl replied under the same title in the following volume of the same periodical. Then there appeared, in the same place, Böhm-Bawerk's 'Ein Zwischenwort zur Werttheorie', later Dietzel's 'Zur klassischen Wert-und Preistheorie', *loc. cit.* 3 Folge, Vol. 1, and as an answer to the latter Böhm-Bawerk's 'Wert, Kosten und Grenznutzen', *loc. cit.* Vol. 3, the most important polemical performance of the Austrian School.

with the classical economists was maintained by him merely because he completely re-interpreted their doctrines. The change in the point of view which took place was in consequence so much the more complete and unopposed, although it was only P. H. Wicksteed who definitely followed the doctrine of marginal utility and outspokenly rejected the classical economists.[1]

Then the majority of the Dutch[2] and several of the Swedish and Danish theorists turned to the marginal utility theory, and it also became alive and effective in France[3], where it led to a revival of theoretical work. Furthermore, it was particularly in America[4] and in Italy[5] that a rich text-book literature of the theory of marginal utility developed.

For the development of matters in Germany it was of great importance that v. Philippovich supported the theory of marginal utility in his compendium through which it became known also to those economists who were not quite so interested in theory as such. Its success in countries outside Germany worked in its favour also, even if this success was bound to appear smaller than in fact it was to the non-theorist who has to rely on the basic statements of the various authors. Nevertheless the circle of its

[1] *The Alphabet of Economic Science*, *Essay on the Co-ordination of the Laws of Distribution*, *The Commonsense of Political Economy*. The position of Edgeworth can be characterized in a similar way to that of Marshall, though he stood a shade nearer to the classical economists. Most English theorists could be mentioned here, in particular A. C. Pigou.

[2] N. G. Pierson must be described as the leading economist. *Leerboek der staathuishoudkunde*, 1884–90; English translation under the title *Manual of Political Economy*. He was followed by Heymans, d'Aulnis, Beaujon, Harts, Falkenburg, Verijn Stuart and others.

[3] Gide, Landry, Ch. Rist.

[4] Amongst the American economists some like Fetter, Patten, Fisher are unconditional supporters of the marginal utility theory, others like Clark, Seligman, Commons, Davenport, Seager support it with unimportant qualifications. So does in fact Taussig, while Ely and others stand further away. As an opponent we might mention Veblen among others.

[5] The leading economists, above all Pareto and Pantaleoni are 'marginal utility theorists'. To this group belong also Graziani, Ricca-Salerno, Cossa, Mazzola, Conigliani, Barone, opponents are: Loria, Supino and others. Compare v. Schullern-Schrattenhofen, *Die theoretische Nationalökonomie Italiens in neuester Zeit*, 1891.

unconditional supporters in Germany was also entirely limited to the Austrian school (we mention in addition R. Zuckerkandl, R. Meyer, V. Mataja, E. Sax, R. Schüller).

Yet opposition on principle diminished, even if it has continued until today. In the small circle of German theorists some writers evolved that point of view which has been described correctly as 'eclectic'. This view can roughly be summed up as follows: the basic element of the theory of marginal utility was incorporated into a theory of value and partly also into a theory of price; for the rest, however, people held on to older conceptions. Here belongs A. Wagner, *Allgemeine oder theoretische Volkswirtschaftslehre*, 1876, 79, p. 92, *et. seq.*, who describes Rodbertus and Schäffle as those authors who stood nearest to him and who assigns to the heory of marginal utility a limited sphere.

So far we had little opportunity to talk of Schäffle. In fact it is difficult to place this powerful personality correctly in a history of economic doctrines. He absorbed most of the trends of his age in the fields of *Sozialpolitik*, history and sociology, and he also was a theoretical economist. In everything he did he was successful in his presentation, original in his formulations and systematic in his treatment, but he was not really a profound scholar. (Compare Schmoller, *Zur Literaturgeschichte der Staats-und Sozialwissenschaften*, Fabian-Sagal, *Albert Schäffle und seine theoretisch-ökonomischen Lehren.*) His main works (*Nationalökonomie*, 1861, *Gesellschaftliches System der menschlichen Wirtschaft*, 1867 and 1873, *Kapitalismus und Sozialismus*, 1870 and 1878, *Bau und Leben des sozialen Körpers*, 1875–8, 1896–7) have had an extremely stimulating effect, but it would be difficult to quote from them even a single permanent result, even a single interpretation that was at once original and fruitful.

The point of view of Lexis, *Allgemeine Volkswirtschaftslehre*, 1910, is also eclectic. He approaches the whole of theory with the same scepticism which is noticeable in his attitude to economic history in his work on the French export premiums, and he passes as quickly as possible over the basic theoretical problems to practical questions. In his text-book on Economics we find the theory of marginal utility added on to a structure which was essentially based on classical material or at least which consists of material which he had derived from his criticism of the classical economists. Diehl also, whose most important works have already been mentioned, belongs here (compare also his contribution in the *Schmollerfestgabe*), likewise v. Bortkiewicz. These examples must suffice. All in all a picture of an uncomfortable period of transition with a preponderantly critical disposition unfolds itself. The positive elan, as far as it existed at all, was mostly used up in attempts to find new foundations for the theory, but we cannot go more deeply into the latest phase of this development.

The general picture of the economic process as presented by the supporters of the theory of marginal utility, that is, in particular their description of the different types of members of the economy and their roles, all this is not substantially different from the classical picture. The theory of marginal utility, however, places the main emphasis on a complex of problems which the classical economists passed over too lightly, namely, the foundations for the determination of value and price. The classical economists, especially Ricardo and his group, were content to point to the effect of free competition and to maintain that from it resulted a definite law which determined the *amount* of value and price. Armed with these conceptions they immediately seized some great objective facts and tendencies, such as the price of corn, the number of workers, etc., which were determined by the law of populations or the law of diminishing returns from land, and which they tried to combine into a picture of the concrete laws which governed prices and incomes.

The theory of marginal utility attempted in the first place to investigate in detail the various groups of events which result from the basic facts of economic activity, without at first introducing additional concrete data. It placed the explanation of the nature of price determination and of the various forms of income into her forefront and headed therefore in a different direction from the beginning. Thus a different and much 'purer' economics originated which contains much less concrete and factual material and accotdingly offers considerably fewer summarized practical conclusions, but is immeasurably more firmly founded. Also from this new point of view the reciprocal relation between the various units in the economy was revealed far more clearly and it became more evident that many rigid causal chains of the classical economists could not be accepted. Moreover, their naïve conviction that only the great objective facts were important, while the process of price determination contained nothing very relevant, was shown to be unfounded.

The theory of marginal utility in addition completely abandoned those averages and approximations which had given such a semblance of precision to the classical doctrine. All this means that the classical picture of economics was not merely elaborated and supplemented but that it was in fact corrected. This correction, however, rendered some classical conclusions irrelevant and proved others as false, although it was not possible to replace them by similarly brief propositions. The representatives of the theory of marginal utility from their point of view perceived much more clearly than the classical economists had done, that conclusions depend on the concrete data which themselves must be derived from case to case from the material of the facts of place and time and cannot be established once and for all in a definite manner. This knowledge, which certainly demands humility from us, assumed in the parlance of the opponents, the form of a charge that the theory of marginal utility was 'barren'.

The second essential difference between the new and the old theory is the abandonment of the conception of the quantity of labour as the factor which regulates and measures the value of commodities—not to mention other 'cost theories'—and the emphasis which was given to the consideration and the development of the conception of value in use. This shifting of emphasis on to the doctrine of 'subjective values' in economics produced four advantages. It is more correct because the various cost theories are valid at best only approximately and never base the phenomenon of cost on those facts which really explain it. It is simpler because the labour value theory in particular necessitates a number of auxiliary constructions which now simply disappear. It is more general because all cost theories refer in the first place only to those commodities which have been produced in free competition, and in part to those commodities only which can be increased at will. Furthermore, they are valid only for periods of a certain duration. The doctrine of subjective value, on the other hand, comprises in an equal manner all commodities, whether produced under monopoly conditions or not, whether capable of being increased or not, and for long as well as for short periods. Finally, the theory of marginal utility makes economic conclusions more relevant, because for most problems the conditions in which wants are satisfied, and the way in which these wants change, are more important than changes in the quantity of labour which is contained in the commodities the consumption of which produces this satisfaction.

The theory of marginal utility accepts value in use as a fact of individual psychology. It is basically nothing but the law of satiated wants as formulated by Bernoulli, Gossen, Jennings and other 'forerunners'.[1] This method of starting from a fact of individual psychology led to two groups of objections. Firstly, the general objections to individualism and atomism were levelled especially against this school. In this respect an adequate distinction between political individualism, the view that individuals are independent causes of social phenomena which represent merely a resultant of these causes, and the mere method of starting from the individual for purposes of pure economics, was not made. The representatives of the theory of marginal utility reacted to these objections in different ways. Some ignored them altogether, others tried to deny their validity or importance in principle, still others attempted to take them into account by stressing the social element as much as possible.

Amongst the latter we must mention in particular the group which employs the term of 'social use value' and stresses the valuations of the social groups as opposed to those of the individual (v. Wieser, similarly the school of Clark). We cannot go into the contents of these discussions. Let us merely mention that there is a special variety of this charge, represented by the assertion which is often made in Marxist quarters, that the theory of marginal uti-

[1] This law was—rightly or wrongly—associated with the 'psycho-physical' basic law. On this point compare M. Weber, 'Die Grenznutzenlehre und das psychophysische Grundgesetz', *Archiv für Sozialwissenschaft*, 1908.

lity is nothing but a description of the mentality of the employer and that by its individualist point of departure its representatives make it impossible for themselves to see the great objective conditions and results of the economic process.[1]

Secondly, because of its starting point the theory of marginal utility became associated with psychological and philosophical Hedonism. Its representatives are often called 'hedonists'. This first of all implies the charge of having dragged psychological considerations into economics at all and, furthermore, of being concerned with an antiquated and erroneous psychology. Most of the marginal utility theorists tried to point out in reply that they did not turn into 'psychologists' merely by starting from a fact of psychological experience, others tried to avoid any statements of a psychological character altogether and to proceed strictly from basic economic facts that could be observed from the outside.[2] Only a few reveal a relation to utilitarianism, amongst them above all Jevons. We could, however, replace his utilitarian creed by a protest against utilitarianism without having to abandon one single economic conclusion of his. There was an additional charge against the kind of 'psychology' which was found in the works of the marginal utility theorists: this charge refers to its rationalist character. There is a parallel development in the modern school of professional psychologists (Meinong, Ehrenfels and others).

[1] Yet, as Bortkiewicz in his work on Marx, which we quoted above, justly points out, however 'insipid' the capitalist manner of calculation may be, its importance for capitalist reality is no less for that. Furthermore, we have already repeatedly stressed the fact that Marx' argumentation depends also on definite assumptions regarding individual behaviour and that these assumptions can be expressed most naturally in the language of individual psychology.

[2] Thus Pareto, Barone, Auspitz, Lieben and others. Dietzel declared already in his reply to Wieser that the marginal utility theory as 'psychology' did not belong into economics. Compare on this point Wieser, 'Das Wesen und der Hauptinhalt der theoretischen Nationalökonomie', *Schmoller's Jahrb.* 1911, Böhm-Bawerk in the third edition of his *Positive Theorie*, 1912, p. 310, *et. seq.*, 'Hedonismus und Werttheorie' and 'Wertgrössen und Gefühlsgrössen'. Most of the objections against the psychology of the marginal utility theory are summed up in Lifschitz' treatise: *Zur Kritik der Böhm-Bawerkschen Werttheorie*, 1908; compare for this my review in the *Zeitschrift für Volkswirtschaft, Sozialpolitik und Verwaltung*, 1910.

Within the theory of marginal utility itself a rift revealed itself which went back to a classical influence, centred round Senior and Cairnes. While the Austrian school took merely the element of the use value of products as the basis of their explanation, Jevons already placed next to it the element of 'disutility of labour' as a second factor in the formation of the value of commodities in connection with his basic conception of economics as calculus of pleasure and pain. And some of the later thinkers, especially Marshall, further added the element of 'having to wait', Senior's abstinence. This conception prevailed in England and America (cf. besides Marshall also the article by Edgeworth: 'Professor Böhm-Bawerk on The Ultimate Standard of Value', *Economic Journal*, 1897, and Clark: 'The Ultimate Standard of Value', *Yale Review*, 1892), but with these authors it is essentially based on the same foundations as is the pure theory of use value, even if without doubt we can discover in it remnants of the cost theory. Only for the problem of interest does this perhaps involve a considerable difference.[1]

In connection with the discussion about the admissibility or possibility of introducing psychological factors into economics there stood the question of a standard of value. This question became essential as soon as the theorists saw the excellent objective measure of labour vanish. Even before Smith people had discussed the question of a standard of exchange value and it had been recognized that there could be no standard that was unchangeable in itself. All the classical writers taught this, while the old supporters of the theory of value in use, as e.g. Say, insisted on equating the exchange value of a commodity simply with the quantity of goods which it was possible to obtain for it in the market. It was, however, simply considered impossible to measure the value in use, although in practice everybody definitely compares values of commodities with each other. The psychological theory of value now seemed to demand such a standard of value in use also in economic theory. Against this doubts were raised whether it was substantially possible to measure 'quantities of intensity' and in particular whether valuations of different people could actually be compared. Yet

[1] Cf. Böhm, Bawerk, 'Exkurs' IX in the third edition of the *Positive Theorie*.

there is really no need for such a comparison and in measuring the valuations of one person it is quite possible to proceed merely from facts that can be observed if we start from the following formulation: The value of a quantity of a commodity for somebody is measured by that quantity of another commodity which makes the choice between both a matter of indifference to the economic individual. (Fisher, *Mathematical Investigations into the Theory of Prices*, 1892.) This method of basing the measurement of values on acts of choice of the individuals gained more and more adherents (Pareto, Boninsegni and others). Yet it is possible to overcome the difficulties of the problem also in a different way.[1]

The primary fact with which the theory of marginal utility is concerned and in which its fundamental achievement consists and on which everything else is based, is the proof that in spite of appearances to the contrary the factor of wants and as a result from this the utility character of commodities determine all individual occurrences in the economy. At first it was necessary to deal with the old antinomy of values, the opposition between utility and value. This had already been done. The distinctions between categories of want and the incitement of want, between the total value of a store and the value of partial quantities of which the store held by the economic individual is composed, help to overcome this opposition. In this lies the importance of the conception of 'marginal utility'.[2] Thus all facts relating to the determination of prices could be explained with the help of the basic principle. It is true, however, that there never had been any doubt that those facts on which the 'demand side' of the problem of price is based could be explained with its help and this had usually been considered as self-evident. But it was only the theory of marginal utility which based the 'supply side' of the problem on it and conceived costs as phenomena of value. In this respect the decisive achievement—mostly overlooked by the critics—lay in the proof that the esti-

[1] Compare Cuhel, *Zur Lehre von den Bedürfnissen*, 1907; on this Exkurs X in Böhm-Bawerk's treatise, quoted above.

[2] In German *Grenznutzen*, in English the term 'final utility' was formerly used, in French *rareté, utilité limite*. Pareto coined the expression *ophelimité elementaire*, in order to exclude the secondary meaning of the terms 'value' and 'utility'.

mation of commodities according to their costs, which is so predominant in economic life, is merely an expedient abbreviation of the real correlation, that this correlation is explained with the help of the element of value in use, that the calculations of the entrepreneur are merely the reflection of valuations on the part of the consumers, and that in cases in which somebody estimates a commodity according to the value in use of commodities which he can obtain for it in the market—subjective exchange value—the 'exchangeability' and with it the subjective exchange value is based on alternative estimates of the value in use. This led to a uniform explanation of all occurrences in the exchange economy with the help of one single principle and in particular also to a classification of the relation between costs and prices.[1] The classical law of costs—the proposition of the tendency for costs and returns to equate in free competition—only now received a cogent justification and its deeper meaning. If, therefore, the interaction of supply and demand has been compared to the co-operation of the two blades of a pair of scissors (Marshall) no opposition to the theory of marginal utility was implied as long as both were based on the same factor, that is, as long as the costs of any production were equated with the resulting utility of those productions which would otherwise have been possible with the same means of production (opportunity cost, displacement cost).[2] Yet as most

[1] It has been said repeatedly that the theory of marginal utility because it starts from the valuation of given quantities of goods disregards the process of production and is unable to explain how these quantities come into being. Yet the assumption of given quantities of goods merely serves as an introductory demonstration of the law of marginal utility. At a further stage these quantities of goods become unknown factors, and the investigation of the causes that determined them becomes the main problem, as appears particularly clearly in the system of Walras. It has further been said that the theory of marginal utility makes the value of the various goods depend only on their quantity and neglects the influence which the existence of other goods exercises on them. This likewise is only true as far as preliminary discussions are concerned. At a further stage the value of any commodity is treated as an element in the total economic situation of every individual (cf. in particular Marshall and Pareto). Neither does the fact that supply, demand and price mutually influence each other constitute on objection against the theory of marginal utility, although it is usually stated as such.

[2] Cf. Davenport, *Value and Distribution*, 1908.

English authors base the 'supply side' of the problem on the independent element of disutility of labour and postponement of enjoyment, the formulation referred to is usually put forward in the form of an objection. The material difference, however, from the pure theory of value in use, revealed by this attitude, is, as has been said already, extremely small.

On this basis there emerged above all a solid theory of price which had been lacking in the system of the classical economists. It was created in particular by Böhm-Bawerk and Walras and has been carefully elaborated ever since. We cannot describe its contents here and should merely like to emphasize that apart from numerous individual achievements (theory of monopoly, theory of devolution of taxes, of international values and of transport tariffs) it helps us to obtain a comprehensive survey of the economic process, in comparison with which the classical theory merely has the significance of having stressed some special cases one-sidedly. It described for the first time the interaction of individuals and functions within the organism of the national economy according to clear concepts and on the basis of a uniform principle of explanation. It is true that it is far less 'concrete' than the theory of the classical economists had been and that only a collection of facts, particularly of a statistical nature, can give to it that factual precision which is required if we want to gain more than a general understanding of the nature of the economic process. So far there have only been beginnings in this direction but the theoretical structure has almost been completed. Really important controversies no longer exist within this theory of price.

The basic idea of the theory of marginal utility does not force its supporters to adopt a definite position with regard to the problem of money and can be employed within the framework of any theory of money. The special features of the problem of money make it possible for different solutions to emerge from the same complex of principles. C. Menger (Article 'Geld' in *Handwörterbuch der Staatswissenschaften*) developed the theory of money in one direction—we may employ a terminology which has become customary and describe it as 'metallic'—Jevons, Pareto and many others also hold this position. Yet in addition a completely different theory of money developed (Walras, Wieser) in which the material value of money plays an entirely subordinate part and which explains the way in which money determines value as the result of its function in the organism of the national economy. The quantity theory of money had already attempted to do this in its way but it merely stated a rigid approximative formula of little explanatory value. The aforementioned new theory, on the other hand, tried to go to the root of the matter in a way similar to the modern theory of value which stands in quite an analogous relation to the classical law of price. This new theory had contacts with a general movement in this field. Gradually and silently—in England, e.g., almost entirely through gradual changes in the oral teaching—new conceptions established themselves which have produced a rich harvest. Amongst these we may mention Knapp's *Staatliche Theorie des Geldes*, 1905, which attracted the attention of the public at large. While the systematic literature of the subject, as shown by the works of Helfferich, Martello, Laughlin, Foville and others, predominantly maintains the old point of view, the discussion of currency problems—Lexis, Lotz and others—gradually brought the majority of economists nearer to the new point of view.

The problem of distribution is the most important one in the new economic theory as it had been in the old one. Here the theory of marginal utility established its basic conception uniformly in opposition to the special explanations of each separate branch of income given by the classical economists. In doing so it took over the inheritance of the 'theory of the productive services'. The latter, however, had foundered on the objections that the 'shares' of the various factors of production are inextricably mixed up in the product, or that it is altogether impossible to talk of such 'shares', because in fact all means of production are equally important for the production of the commodity, and that the productive services have nothing to do with the rewards of the owners of the factors of production. Now, on the other hand, it was possible to prove with the help of the marginal analysis that we can attach a precise economic sense to the expression 'product of a factor of production' and that in fact in everyday economic life a distinction is made between such shares of the various factors of production.

The theory of price then did the rest by proving that the value of the productive contribution of the various factors of production really forms the basis for the formation of incomes. Nevertheless the objection that individual contributions of the factors of production cannot really be distinguished has sometimes been maintained until our own days. On the whole, however, we can say that the explanation of the branches of income and of their size with the help of the 'marginal product' of the factors of production has become an undebatable commonplace, especially in the American, English and Italian literature, but also in that of France.

Matters are different with the theory of 'imputation' (Zurechnung) which is characteristic of the Austrian wing of the supporters of the theory of marginal utility (Menger, Wieser, Böhm-Bawerk). This theory is supposed to form the bridge between the values and prices of products and those of the means of production and to indicate the rules according to which the value of the product is as it were reflected in the value of the means of production. Although we do not find in the other groups of the marginal utility school investigations of this point and the term 'imputation' is mentioned by them only in passing or even in a hostile way, we find everywhere, nevertheless, the heart of the matter, e.g. in Marshall's 'principle of substitution' and in Clark's 'law of variation'.

There are hardly any really serious differences about these basic principles, however little the fundamental unity appears on the surface.[1] There are such differences, however, on one point, which

[1] There is essential agreement on the theory of wages and rent. Wages equal the marginal product of labour. The theory of ground-rent indeed did not completely emancipate itself from the form which Ricardo had given to it, but the characteristic statement that rent does not enter into price lost its significance, so that even in authors who formally clung to Ricardo, as did Marshall, the connection between productivity of the land and rent is established. In modern theory the conception of rent plays a large part. Since indeed the classical economists had already applied the marginal analysis to the ground-rent the modern theory of distribution sometimes appears under the aspect of a generalization of the classical theory of ground-rent, with the difference that the law of diminishing marginal utility replaced or supple-

is actually vital for our entire insight into the social process of the economy and the economic structure of society, the problem of interest on capital. In 1884 there appeared Böhm-Bawerk's critical work which established not only the untenable but also the superficial character of the existing explanations of interest and opened a new era for the theory of interest. This book and the one entitled *Positive Theorie*, which followed four years later, trained numerous theorists of interest and hardly a single one remained unaffected by them. Of all the works on the theory of marginal utility these two volumes had the deepest and widest effect. We find the traces of their influence in the way in which almost all theorists of interest phrased their questions and proceeded to answer them. There are signs of this influence even in those writers who rejected the concrete solution of the problem of interest as offered by Böhm-Bawerk. This solution is based on the fundamental idea that the phenomenon of interest can be explained by a discrepancy between the values of present and future consumer goods. This discrepancy rests on three facts: first, on the difference between the present and the future level of supplies available for the members of the economy, secondly, on the fact that a future satisfaction of wants stands much less vividly before people's eyes than an equal but present satisfaction. In consequence, economic activity reacts less strongly to the prospect of future satisfaction than to that of present enjoyment and the individual members of the economy are in certain circumstances willing to buy present enjoyment with one that is greater in itself but lies in the future. The discrepancy between present and future values is, thirdly, based on the fact that the possession of goods ready to be enjoyed makes it unnecessary for the economic individuals to provide for their subsistence by

---

mented the law of diminishing returns. This is particularly true of the American theory. Compare Johnson, 'Rent in Modern Economic Theory', *American Economic Assoc. Publ.* 1902); Fetter, 'The Passing of the Old Rent Concept, *Quarterly Journal of Economics*, 1901; Clark, 'Distribution as Determined by a Law of Rent' (*ibidem*, Vol. 5). We might in addition mention the application of the conception of rent to that of the subjective gain in utility derived from exchange and production. (Marshall's consumer surplus.)

producing for the moment, e.g. by a primitive search for food. The possession of such goods enables them to choose some methods of production which are more profitable but are more time-consuming: the possession of goods ready to be enjoyed in the present guarantees, as it were, the possession of more such goods in the future.

In this 'third reason' for the phenomenon of interest there are contained two elements: First, the establishment of a technical fact which so far had been unknown to the theorists, namely that the prolongation of the period of production, the adoption of 'detours' of production, makes it possible to obtain a greater return which is more than proportionate to the time employed. Secondly, the thesis that this technical fact is also an independent cause of an increase in value of consumption goods which are in existence at any given time.

Interest as form of income then originates in the price struggle between the capitalists on the one side, who must be considered as merchants who offer goods which are ready for consumption, and landlords and workers on the other. Because the latter value present goods more highly and because the possible use of present stocks of consumer goods for a more profitable extension of the period of production is practically unlimited, the price struggle is always decided in favour of the capitalists. In consequence, landlords and workers receive their future product only with a deduction, as it were, with a discount for the present.

The achievement which this formulation contains was epoch-making and a great deal of the theoretical work of the last twenty years has been devoted to a discussion of it and to its criticism. To those who have accepted this theory to its full extent, e.g. Pierson, Gide, Taussig (lately: *Principles of Economics*, 1912), must be added the different groups of all those who have learned from it and have borrowed some of its ideas. Thus Fisher *Capital and Interest*, 1906, *Rate of Interest*, 1908 and Fetter, *Principles of Economics*, 1904, took the 'psychological depreciation' of future satisfaction of wants as a basis for their explanation of interest and approached Jevons' point of view in this way. They elaborated further the theory of interest into a general theory of returns from wealth, for which the foundations are contained in Böhm-Bawerk's work as well.

Others, like John B. Clark, *Distribution of Wealth*, 1899, and Wieser, held on to the theory of productivity but attempted to give it a different foundation—both in different ways. Still others united the basic elements of various explanations of interest into a new picture of the phenomenon. (Thus Marshall combined the theory of abstinence and productivity and Carver, *Distribution of Wealth*, proceeded slightly differently.) Apart from these there are quite a few authors who hold on to the older methods of explaining interest. There can, however, be no question here of trying to present a tolerably complete survey of even the most important intellectual currents.

Less happened in the field of the theory of the profit of the entrepreneur. The discussion moved chiefly within the framework of ideas which have been indicated already in the preceding section. The rest of the theoretical work was devoted to specialized questions and was not directly concerned with the way in which the basic theoretical problems moved. Amongst them the question of economic crises stands out as the most important. After C. Juglar, *Des crises commerciales*, 1889, had recognized the cyclical movement of economic life as the essential phenomenon and had discovered the immediate causes of the crises in the period of boom which precedes every economic crisis, this idea became the basis for the work devoted to the problem of crisis. Most modern performances in this field, especially that of Spiethoff, are based on similar foundations.

The vehemence of the controversies about methods and doctrines in our discipline often seems to interrupt the continuity of development. This vehemence can be explained partly by the inherent character of economics and the political interest which people take in economic theses that are either really or allegedly economic; partly it results from the fact that determined scientific work in this field is of comparatively recent date. Nevertheless it is surprising how comparatively little the controversy of the day influenced the course of quiet studies at the time.

If we look through the veil of the arguments employed in the struggle we see much less of the contrasts which are usually formulated on principle with such acerbity. We see that these contrasts are not always irreconcilable materially and that the different schools do not easily overcome each other to the point of annihilation. The Physiocrats already wanted basically the same things which we want today and if we look at the essence of the matter and not at the form employed to express it, it is often difficult for us to find a strong enough formulation of the *objective* party position which corresponds to the bitterness of the struggle. Thus even our science does not lack an organic development. Grown out of the instinctive knowledge of the basic facts of economic life it consolidated itself in connection with the ideas that were formed by the practical experiences of the eighteenth century. Moreover, what had been achieved was slowly and steadily extended, in spite of all attempts to base our science on entirely new foundations. This extension was not particularly fast and all appearances to the contrary turned out to be deceptive on every occasion—in this field also really great achievements were rare. Neither, however, did it ever stagnate. Much strength was wasted by people groping their way and by trying out different approaches. This was inevitable because an economist has very rarely other completely assenting economists for his public. In consequence everybody has to fight for his position and has to furnish his contribution to economic thought with a long polemical introduction. This was so in the early stages of all sciences and will remain so for a long time to come in our science. Phases of development cannot be passed over in the case of an organic body any more than in the case of political, social or scientific bodies. Nevertheless the misdirection of energy will abate as time goes on and then it will be easier to survey the basic outlines of the work done in the field of social science during the last 150 years and to discover its underlying unity.

INDEX